MOM, DAD, I'M AN ATHEIST

MOM, DAD, I'M AN ATHEIST

The Guide to Coming Out as a Non-believer

DAVID G McAFEE

dangerous™
little books

First Published in Great Britain 2012
by Dangerous Little Books

© Copyright David G McAfee

© Author photograph by Sharona Belles
© Cartoons by Chuck Harrison

"For many people, figuring out that the supernatural claims of religions don't hold up to honest analysis is relatively easy. It's the next step—sharing this conclusion with mom and dad—that often proves to be the most difficult of all. Fortunately, David G. McAfee has produced an invaluable contribution to all nonbelievers who find they must navigate that most treacherous minefield known as the religious family. With deep wisdom and sincere compassion, McAfee explores the challenges and suggests the best tactics, while also offering much-needed encouragement for those who may find the journey difficult. It is because he understands that the goal is freethought, self-expression, and the preservation of important relationships, that this book is a precious resource."

Guy P. Harrison, author of *Race and Reality* and
50 Simple Questions for Every Christian

Acknowledgements

To my mom and dad, who never let differences of opinion stand in the way of treating me with love and respect.

Thank you to those who contributed to this work their personal narratives, without which this book wouldn't be possible. Special thanks to Holly Samel, Nickolas Johnson, Elizabeth Rouse, Hugh Kramer, Cleta Darnell, Jason Sciple, and Julia Sciple.

Contents

Contents

Preface

"Intolerance is the natural concomitant of strong faith; tolerance grows only when faith loses certainty; certainty is murderous."
— Will Durant (November 5, 1885 – November 7, 1981)

When you hear the term "coming out" applied to atheism or non-religiosity, you might jump to a few conclusions... you might assume that the act only applies to those who are *new* to non-belief, or that it is a one-off personal event only involving close family, or that it is only an issue for those raised in fundamentally religious homes — in each of these cases, there is certainly more than meets the eye.

I am by no means new to atheism or non-religiosity — and, in fact, I was never a believer. But even I had to "come out" as an atheist at one point or another because theism and religiosity are the assumed points of view in many cultures, including mine. That assumption is interesting in itself because religion is a learned behavior, unlike non-belief; all people are born not believing in a god or gods, and only come to believe in such entities once they've been taught the idea by others — so, atheism is the "default" position. Despite this fact, in many regions of the world, the simple act of being openly atheist is punishable by death. In other countries, like the United States of America, atheism isn't punishable within the legal system, but discrimination comes in other forms. This is why, even if you've been a non-believer for your entire life, being "open" about it will almost always result in — at the very least — some awkward discussions and forced explanations between you and the people with whom you interact regularly. It is my hope that this guide will provide tips and resources for even the most seasoned heathens.

Being an "out" atheist since childhood, I've experienced my share of disappointed looks and the occasional intellectual misunderstanding with my religious family members. But it wasn't until I was applying to graduate school for the Religious Studies department at University of California, Santa Barbara, that I realized that being a non-believer can have real effects on my professional and educational lives, in addition to those I'd already experienced in my personal life. Being open about my non-belief and my secular activism resulted in my being denied entry to the MA/PhD program and the discrimination grievance that followed. I quickly realized that it is not just family that one worries about in these situations. My experience is more thoroughly documented in **Chapter Three:** *Atheist Activist with an Axe to Grind*.

Coming out as an atheist means more than simply telling religious family members about a lack of faith or a loss of faith; in many cases, even people who come from non-religious upbringings have to confront the issue with friends, colleagues, acquaintances, and, in my case, all of the above. As such, coming out is not necessarily a one-time matter, but should instead be considered an ongoing process throughout one's lifetime. As is the case with "coming out" in the LGBT (Lesbian, Gay, Bisexual, Transgender) community, it is never enough to simply come out once to your family. If you truly want to be an out-of-the-closet non-believer and, perhaps, in the process help other closeted atheists who may be afraid to voice their skepticism,

it is sometimes necessary to confront those in day-to-day life who may assume your religiosity or project their religious ideologies onto you.

While those coming from fundamentally religious homes or communities may suffer more deeply from religious oppression and therefore be helped tremendously by the resources and advice provided in this guide, a fundamentally religious upbringing is not a prerequisite for "coming out," and people from non-religious upbringings still face difficulties with being honest about a lack of belief in a god or gods. Even in relaxed religious homes, the negative stigma associated with the word "atheist" alone can cause confusion and potential friction between loved ones.

In *Chapter Eleven: Testimonials*, I have included stories by non-believers from a variety of backgrounds who tell their stories of de-conversion. But, while this guide was written with input from several contributing authors who experienced coming out to less-than-supportive families or friends, it is important to remember that no two situations are identical — and what works for one person, does not necessarily work for another. Like many issues that involve familial transparency, being openly non-religious has different consequences for everyone. And, in dangerous scenarios, it is important to seek professional guidance or counseling. Please see *Chapter Twelve: Extreme Situations* for further information on that front.

This work is intended to give advice to those who have been afraid to talk about their non-belief and encourage familial honesty, but also to help "out" atheists deal with the daily interactions and frequently asked questions they may experience in day-to-day life. The resources compiled in *Chapter Fifteen: Resources & Support* are useful for all those who are non-religious and hope to establish a sense of community with freethinkers, raise children in a secular environment, or simply gain more information about secularism and free thought.

Author's Note: Born Atheist

"It is an interesting and demonstrable fact, that all children are atheists and were religion not inculcated into their minds, they would remain so."
— Ernestine Louise Rose (January 13, 1810 - August 4, 1892)

To properly understand this guide to coming out as a non-believer, some might wish to learn more about the particular context in which I, as a secular author, am writing. In **Chapter Eleven:** *Testimonials*, you'll read six stories from atheists who wished to share their de-conversion testimonials for the benefit of those who may be facing difficulties in their own coming out process. Here, I do the same:

The way I see it, *everybody* is born an atheist and, without submersion into religion as a child, we would most likely maintain that position... more often than not, however, this is not the case. In most instances, a child is taught early on that their parents' religion is the Truth — and all others are *evil*. This mindset is rarely shaken and those beliefs are often passed to further generations. Luckily for me, that didn't happen.

I don't remember a particular time in my life in which I *believed* in the validity of a particular religious tradition. But, eventually, even I had to break the news to my family and become open regarding my secular mindset. My parents were not always religious people; they may have abused substances religiously — but, when I was very young, church was probably the last thing on their minds. When I was two years old, my parents divorced and began their separate lives pursuing drugs to feed their addictions; thankfully, my grandmother volunteered to care for me until my mother or father could afford (financially and emotionally) to raise me. She never mistreated me or abused me, but she was the first person in my life to introduce me to religion and the authority of the Christian church. My grandparents with whom I spent the majority of my early childhood considered themselves Fundamentalist Baptist Christians — and I was raised in a way that, they thought, would encourage similar ideologies in me.

When I was a bit older — around six years old — I went to a Christian church with my grandparents; this was my first *real* experience with a religious institution. The church, located in a small town in Northern California, considered itself "non-denominational," and the service usually consisted of a pastor reciting well-chosen biblical passages for about an hour and providing some minor inspirational interpretations. I attended sporadically but, needless to say, I was not *moved* by the experience and didn't take the idea of church seriously. Even though this doctrine was being force-fed to me for as long as I could remember, I always had questions about its veracity — questions that, I quickly learned, were considered inappropriate to ask. My grandmother was a self-described traditional, god-fearing, Christian woman — it wasn't until much later that I would realize the closed-mindedness that this mindset bred in her and others over time. She saw that I was not excited about attending church on a regular basis and, at around age eight, she mandated that I attend a weekly children's class at the same church in an attempt to force more involvement and encourage my participation within the "House of God." I remember my first day at this Sunday school very well; I remember that my younger step-sister was there with me in a classroom-like setting learning about Jesus Christ and his message, obviously at a superficial level that could be more easily absorbed by young children. I also remember the tactics utilized by the "teachers" to keep the attention of the children and get us excited about church — usually this consisted of giving gifts of candy and prizes for active participation. I do not doubt that the *intentions* of these people were positive but, in hindsight, I cannot help but see the gifts as a type of mild bribery in exchange for the willing indoctrination of a child. After we earned a certain amount of "Bible Bucks," which were awarded for correctly answering trivia questions about the gospels and participating in Christian songs, we could cash in these vouchers for prizes like candy, toys, or even a ten-minute break to play on the trampoline behind the church.

The bus ride to and from Sunday school was the most exciting part of the event for me and my step-sister; we would play games, sing songs, and we were *always* given a lot of candy. My point in telling you this is not to glorify the practice of forcing a religion on a child before they reach the age of reason, but instead to illuminate the *ways* in which this act is carried out within the Christian community and other religious traditions. My step-sister was *always* excited to attend church for the prizes and it didn't take long for this connection to become a subconscious one, which helped foster an extremely positive outlook of church and religion in her mind. For one reason or another, I did not have this reaction — I simply didn't take church or religion seriously. I remember thinking of it more as a pastime or a game to occupy my time on Sunday mornings, acknowledging that the "miracles" portrayed in the biblical texts could not have possibly occurred. There is no point in my past in which I would have considered myself "Christian," or affiliated with any other religion for that matter. But, because my parents became increasingly religious over time and my grandparents had always taken Christianity as God's inherent truth, I was afraid to voice my opinions on the subject. It was this disparity between my family's faith and my lack of faith that spurred my interest in the study of religion. It wasn't until age 13 that I became interested in actively studying the various religious traditions in the world and their effects on society at large. It is because of this curiosity, and my sincere hope to avoid familial confrontation, that I decided to remain silent about my skepticism surrounding Christianity — and all religions. I continued to accompany my family to church on Sundays — as a silent observer. After years of attending the same Christian church nearly every week, however, I had a lot of unanswered questions about the religion's history, principles, and how it became the world's most followed religion. But, out of fear of being ostracized, I remained silent and did not raise my specific concerns to my family, although my lack of participation and general attitude toward church was probably quite telling.

At age 15, long since having decided that I wasn't getting enough information out of the weekly sermons to justify any sort of divine revelation, I decided to read the bible in its entirety to get a more complete picture of what it teaches and, more importantly, why. It is at this time, after seeing first-hand the violent, discriminatory, and hate-filled passages that our pastor had neglected to read aloud, that I decided that not only was I not a Christian, but I was against the notion of organized religion in general. I could have remained silent for years as so many of us do, but instead I decided to confront my family head on. It is at age 15 that I first told my family that I didn't want to go to church anymore because I disagreed with the religion on a fundamental and moral level. I was honest and respectful about my opinions, but that didn't stop them from attempting to *force* my participation in the church — they probably thought they were doing the right thing, trying to "save my soul." I remember them being upset with me at first — as you might expect. But, because of my straightforward and honest attitude, and because I broached the subject rather early in life, it blew over relatively quickly. In short, *they got over it.* From age 15 on it was known to all those in my immediate family that I was a *Religious Conscientious Objector* and, while some of the more closed-minded family members looked down on me for this rather bold announcement, I simply *turned the other cheek.* Now, I am an open atheist in my private and public life and believe that I am truly better off for it. While keeping your opinions on issues related to dogma hidden might help to avoid small confrontations, being honest with yourself and others can be more rewarding in the long term. I truly empathize with those people who are still being forced to hide their non-religiosity from friends and family who might otherwise discriminate against them — and that's the purpose of this book.

I understand that because I never fully *believed* in any deity or religion, my de-conversion and "coming out" isn't as divisive as some of my atheist friends and colleagues. Those who were more invested in church might have a more difficult time sharing their new-found skepticism with friends and family, who are likely enshrined in the same tradition — often with extreme fervor. This includes those non-believers who were once clergymen or preachers or otherwise associated with a religious tradition — this dynamic presents its own set of unique challenges.

But the reason my de-conversion was *not* a traumatic moment in my life is precisely *because* I didn't wait. By telling my family as soon as I was sure that I didn't want to be involved in the church, it became a soon-forgotten aspect to my developing personality — *my family got used to it*. By the time I was 18 years old and I decided to attend school for Religious Studies, nobody in my family or circle of friends was surprised that I was interested in studying the phenomenon of religion from a secular perspective; and, although I catch flak from strangers every once in a while, my true friends and family continue to love and respect me for who I am, regardless of religious and ideological difference — of which there are many.

This is, in my opinion, how it can and *should* be for everybody, provided that you are honest with yourself and others and retain a respectful outlook. In this book, I will outline some steps to make the process easier for you and your loved ones to transition out of religion, provide testimonials from non-believers of all ages who decided to take the enormous step to become open about their lack of belief, and provide helpful information, resources, and support systems for all non-believers. The intention is that these instructions and stories will help people who are being forced to hide their thoughts and feelings from family and friends in a society largely dominated by religion and serve as a reference for those who have already come out as atheists. From dealing with grief from a secular perspective to handling potential clashes in religious worldviews between significant others, this guide offers multiple perspectives from non-religious individuals who have generously donated their anecdotes to help those atheists in similar positions.

Introduction

*"I contend that we are both atheists.
I just believe in one fewer god than
you do. When you understand why you
dismiss all the other possible gods, you
will understand why I dismiss yours."*
— Stephen Roberts

If you're reading this, it is likely that you've decided that you don't *believe*. In a time period in which the overwhelming majority of people not only believe in god(s) — but consider themselves *religious* in one form or another — this can be an important, life-altering decision. While some regions of the world are, as a rule, less religious than others, the power of enculturation has always ensured the theistic majority's place in human society ahead of the others, and being seen as non-religious has long been the source of negative actions and sentiments on the behalf of religious groups. In fact, according to a 2011 study on anti-atheist prejudice sponsored by the American Psychological Association[1], American and Canadian participants said they distrust atheists nearly as much as they distrust rapists when compared to Christians or Muslims.

In some areas of the world, a believer's knee-jerk reaction to one's non-religiosity alone can cause a traumatic situation or confrontation, and it is completely natural to have reservations about becoming an *open* atheist or, because of cultural stigmas, to *consider* yourself an atheist. While you may not believe in an all-knowing God or wish to be part

1   http://www2.psych.ubc.ca/~will/Gervais%20et%20al-%20Atheist%20Distrust.pdf

of any organized religion, the term "atheist" has a negative connotation associated with it that has been historically difficult to overcome. To combat this, non-believers throughout history have created *new* monikers that could be used in order to display non-belief in a more positive manner — without the baggage that is often associated with "atheist." Some of these terms are: Bright, Freethinker, (Secular) Humanist, Non-theist, Agnostic-Atheist, Skeptic, Irreligionist, Rationalist, and Unbeliever. Although the term "atheist" may have begun as a derogatory or pejorative title, the literal meaning of "without god" or "a lack of belief in god(s)" remains important for our purposes and I will continue to use "atheist" and "non-believer" to refer to a non-religious person who is skeptical in regards to a supernatural Creator. An "open" atheist is a person who does not hide the fact that they don't participate in deity worship from their family, friends, and the general public. It is a common misconception that an atheist *necessarily* believes that the existence of a god or gods is *impossible*; the term simply refers to a person who doesn't believe that is the case. In other words, an atheist might simply believe that God, as a concept, is improbable. The definition of "God" also becomes increasingly important here. For "God" in this context, we will ascribe the semi-traditional definition of a supernatural Creator and/or Governor. This description applies to the proposed deities from a wide variety of religions and cultures, and an atheist is simply somebody who doubts the existence of such a being — no more, no less.

Some believers may try to assert that atheism is itself a religion, but this could not be further from the truth. "Atheism" can't be a religion because it's not a belief system — a lack of belief in a god or gods is the only commonality that all

atheists share. I often have to remind believers that I don't pray to any idols, I don't believe in supernatural forces, I don't congregate with other atheists to worship atheism, and I don't tithe to an atheist "church."

The odds are that, if you are a closet atheist or a silent non-believer, your relatives or loved ones probably have a different approach to theological philosophies than you do — hence your hesitation in making your ideas public knowledge. Normally, familial disagreements in a more broad sense would not be such an *enormous* problem, but when it comes to *religious* ideologies, specifically, the ideals and principles are often so firmly held and divisive that disagreements of this nature have been known to end an otherwise flourishing relationship. This is largely because most religions, and therefore most followers of those religions, presuppose the existence of a *Hell* or *hell-like* afterlife in which "sinners" and non-believers reside after *this* life — as opposed to the supposed Heaven or Paradise where believers imagine they will be sent after death. Religions thrive on this mentality because it encourages proselytization and therefore the rapid spread of the tradition. As a result, the religious person far too often sees a non-believer and, instead of judging them based on their actions or simply not judging them at all,[2] they see a sinner whose actions must be corrected to avoid burning in a lake of fire. If you're familiar with Christian teachings, you may be aware that it is often seen as a Christian's moral *duty* to share with the non-religious the "Good Word" of God — and to save the person from an eternity in Hell. That's part of how Christianity became so popular, by successfully permeating other cultures through missionary work.

---

2   NIV 2011 Matthew 7:1-2: "Do not judge, or you too will be judged. For in the same way you judge others, you will be judged, and with the measure you use, it will be measured to you."

Unfortunately, it is this same highly regarded concept of an afterlife that allows misguided religious people to *justify* the mistreatment of those who disagree with their religious ideologies — they are simply trying to *protect* you from eternal damnation in the afterlife by condemning you, insulting you, and even disowning you in *this* life. This is not to say that becoming open about your disbelief is always going to be met with these negative reactions — and, in fact, that is precisely what this work is hoping to prevent — but it is important to understand that, if you experience negative reactions from religious kin, it is probably a result of the religion's teachings and likely not from any personal vendetta or hatred.

The term "coming out" has been applied to the non-religious for years with great success, although it began in reference to homosexuals who disclose their sexual preferences to their family and friends — becoming "openly gay." This act, like becoming an open atheist, is often met with discrimination and familial misunderstanding at extreme levels and is often similarly associated with differing religious beliefs. Because most major religions condemn the act of homosexuality,[3] parents whose child's sexual preferences don't align with what is considered by their religion to be "moral" are forced to deal with the reality (as they perceive it) that their child might suffer in Hell for this behavior. There are a number of programs (sponsored by Christian churches or other religious organizations) that have seen tremendous financial success in preaching religion as the "cure" to homosexual behavior and that one can ensure a place in Heaven by "praying the gay away." Of course, these

---

3   NIV 2011 Leviticus 18:22: "Do not have sexual relations with a man as one does with a woman; that is detestable."

programs do not work. This might be translated into the onslaught of religious literature and church invitations that often occur once an atheist has made their lack of religious convictions open and available to loved ones. The parallels between these two concepts of revelation are numerous, which is why the expression "coming out" is evoked in the subtitle of this work.

It is often difficult for a person who was raised in a religious tradition to deny the teachings they have known since childhood to such an extent that they no longer identify with them — and wish this to be known to others. It is even more difficult for someone to take an active stance against the ideologies or systems taught since childhood — not because the religious arguments are especially convincing or transcendent, but because of the indoctrination that inherently takes place within a religious tradition. Some who are involved in church on a deeper level might also fear political pressures to keep their disbelief a secret. In America, the majority of atheists probably come from a more liberal religious background, for the simple reason that most American Christians practice a form of cultural Christianity — in that they inherit the traditions but don't necessarily understand or care about the intricacies of the religion. In order to expand upon the *cultural* aspects of religiosity, I'd like to quote an essay, entitled *Cultural Christianity*, which was published in my first book: *Disproving Christianity and other Secular Writings:*[4]

> *"...I am referring to a phenomenon that I came across during the course of my research that, to me,*

4   David G. McAfee (2011). Disproving Christianity and Other Secular Writings (2nd edition, revised), pp. 1-6. Dangerous Little Books. ISBN 0-9564276-8-5.

*demonstrates that religion can be something similar
to heritage in that it is passed on from generation to
generation through the parents. For example, people
who have extremely limited knowledge of the Bible or
its implications may still choose to classify themselves
as 'Christians' on the basis that their parents did so.
This phenomenon of children inheriting religion is often overlooked because the perpetrator guilty of indoctrination is not a dictator or cult leader, but their own
parents. When a child is growing up, there is a crucial
period in which he or she begins to ask questions
about the origin of existence — in a religious family,
these questions are typically answered [in accordance
with]... church or Sunday school. Once these beliefs
are instilled in the child, it becomes a part of his or her
identity — so much so that, in many cases, the child
will grow up and forever identify him or herself with
that specific religion without question or skepticism."*

While a religious person may disagree with the term
"indoctrination" in this context, I would argue that it is
especially apt for the discussion of religious instruction of
children. Contrary to popular belief, indoctrination itself
does not imply any negative intentions or motivations;
it simply means that somebody instructs with a bias in
regards to a particular doctrine or ideology (usually in reference a child).[5] By taking a child to church and teaching
them that the rules and ideas learned there are legitimate
and sacred, saying prayers in the home, and teaching the
validity of religious scriptures (even when they sometimes
conflict with modern scientific findings), it is *exactly* this

5   http://www.merriam-webster.com/dictionary/indoctrinate

in which most religious families participate. After being exposed to this indoctrination, as most of us are in one form or another, religion often becomes as firmly held in us as it is in those who raised us, leading to a cycle of similar indoctrination. One rarely questions what he or she has always known to be reality. It is only once a person begins to ask questions regarding the validity of these inherited traditions that they can break free from the cycle of indoctrination and, occasionally, experience a secular breakthrough within a family otherwise inclined toward religion. In some cases, the result is a non-believer who is surrounded by religious loved ones with whom they would like to share their thoughts and concerns, but can't for fear of discrimination and other negative reactions.

It isn't *just* familial honesty and transparency that the non-religious have to deal with in daily life, however. Even those of us whose family members are mainly non-religious, non-present, or otherwise supportive have to deal with coming out as a non-believer in public life with friends, co-workers, and even strangers. In fact, coming out as a non-religious individual should not be thought of as a one-time occurrence, but an ongoing event in which one must continually decide whether or not to speak openly about their lack of faith with people with whom he or she interacts. While it is often considered general etiquette to not discuss politics or religion in order to preserve personal and professional relationships, this does *not* mean that the topic never arises. And it is possible that a religious person presupposes religiosity in conversation and thereby forces the non-believer to either confirm or deny their assumptions. Coming out as an atheist can also apply to these interactions. The notion that informing your family that you are not religious is the entirety of the difficulty with coming out as an atheist could not be further from the truth. Some people choose to remain more silent in the public sphere in regards to religious preferences, which is completely acceptable and understandable; but it is also true that you shouldn't be forced to *hide* your lack of religious ideologies — and having such open discourse shouldn't necessitate a confrontational interaction. After all, why does your lack of religious fervor have to be a source of controversy? Does it actually *affect* anybody but you in any real way? The fact that you don't see sufficient evidence to cultivate a belief in a supernatural Creator, which they happen to believe in, should not be a point of disagreement that leads to an inability to get along or to have comfortable interactions. In fact, many would argue as I have in the past, that "atheism" is the default human setting — as you are not born with knowledge of gods; it is simply from living and being introduced to the concept that a believer adopts theism. At the end of the day, *your* personal feelings and beliefs surrounding religion don't impact the well-being of anybody else and you shouldn't be afraid to be as honest as possible with yourself and others about that fact. Hopefully this guide will allow you to do just that, while maintaining your positive personal relationships with loved ones.

DaVid G. McAfee

Why Come Out?

"It was a high counsel that I once heard given to a young person, 'Always do what you are afraid to do.'"
— Ralph Waldo Emerson (May 25, 1803 – April 27, 1882)

Coming out as an atheist can be scary… in some instances, it can be one of the most difficult things to do: not only are you telling your family that everything they've instilled in you since childhood is bunk, but you are telling them that you choose to disassociate yourself from religious belief altogether. I'll show why that's so inherently confrontational in *Chapter Seven: Confrontation.* Nonetheless, coming out is usually necessary and always something to consider. Overly religious family members and fears of possible bigotry and discrimination might intimidate you, but it is important to remember that the only way to fight such discrimination is to shatter the misconceptions about atheism and secularism. According to the 2007 Pew Forum on Religion and Public Life, only 1.6 percent of the 35,000 respondents described themselves as "atheist," although 6.3 percent described themselves as "secular unaffiliated" and 2.4 percent as agnostic. There are certainly a great deal more than 1.6 percent atheists in America, but only by people coming out and being open about their atheism can that be more accurately represented.

Religious traditions try to guilt you into believing — as if you are somehow a "sinner" since birth — but, all in all, you're probably a great person. So why should being an "atheist" change anything? In many cases, it is because believers often see atheism as "against god." Negative associations with secularism go back as far as religious belief itself: in modern and ancient religions, non-believers are often the "enemy." By being open about your lack of belief, you can show that atheism is not a result of "demons" or "Satan" or any other "evil" thing, but instead it is the result of thinking and research and reason. You can help add to a growing minority of openly atheist individuals bound together by nothing more than one thing: a lack of belief in gods.

By telling people you don't believe, you're making it a bit easier for the next person who has to. You are making it that much easier for the next generation and helping to change the (very false) perception of atheism as something that is anti-god or even pro-evil. More than anything else, coming out as an atheist gives you the opportunity to educate believers — to show them that it is entirely possible to be morally good without believing that we are being policed by an all-knowing deity.

Another reason to come out? *Honesty.* While some people are so fundamentally stuck in their beliefs that they will hate you for disagreeing, the vast majority of believers and non-believers alike are comfortable with disagreement and, when conditions are ideal, they can usually *agree to disagree.* People often appreciate honesty over deceit, even if you are attempting to avoid confrontation.

In some cases, your loved ones will understand that it is natural to disagree and they may even welcome friendly debate. But, even when there is familial tension, it rarely exceeds the downsides of remaining silent. Just by allowing people to assume you are religious (which they undoubtedly will, considering the presence of a religious majority in many areas) does a great disservice to the larger secular community by downplaying how many atheists there actually are. While atheists are larger than some other minority groups, they are for the most part non-present in the political domain in many areas, including and especially the United States.

There is a lot of debate and argument about the word "atheist." Some people are so inherently turned off by the word that they seek alternatives, including misapplying titles like "agnostic" — a term that is not mutually exclusive with "atheist." One of the misconceptions about atheism is that it somehow means someone denies the possibility of a deity. In all actuality, it simply means you don't believe it to be the case — a point that should not be hard to understand with the complete lack of physical evidence that points to the existence of such a being or beings. Even if you're 51 percent sure that there is no magical man in the sky, you are an atheist; and admitting that is the first half of the battle.

Atheist Activist with an Axe to Grind

*"Prejudice, not being founded on reason,
cannot be removed by argument."*
— Samuel Johnson

Being an open atheist since a very young age, I never hid my lack of faith. For that reason, I believe I have the ability to show through my experiences the good *and* bad that comes with being an atheist in a society largely intolerant of non-religiosity. The negative experience to which I'm referring came in the form of discrimination against my atheist activism when applying for the Graduate Program for Religious Studies at the University of California, Santa Barbara, in November of 2010.

I studied at University of California, Santa Barbara, for four years, coming to the campus directly out of high school at age 18. I majored in Religious Studies *and* English and I never had any issue with my lack of religious beliefs in any of my courses. To clarify, I majored in *Religious Studies*, the study of religions from a phenomenological approach, which is not to be confused with Christian *Theology* — the study of Christianity as a fundamental truth. I distinctly remember having a few professors who advocated for the position of one religion or another, but I had never been discriminated against for not believing. As graduation grew near, I decided that I wanted to pursue my education in Religious Studies at UC Santa Barbara in the form of the RGST Graduate Program and Masters/PhD Program, having had a successful and enjoyable tenure there during my undergraduate years. We learned about the historical and cultural aspects of various religions — in some cases even drawing the rightful parallels between the creation myths of the Greeks and Native American and Hindu traditions and those of Abrahamic and Judeo-Christian religions. Although I am not a religious person and, in fact, oppose religion in its more extreme and violent forms, I find the *historical* and *comparative* aspects of Religious Studies extremely helpful in understanding how the human mind works and *why* people believe the things that they do, which is why I've studied religion since a very young age. At a public university, like UCSB, and in a nation bound by a separation of Church and State, like the United States of America, this course of study should be acceptable for somebody of any or no faith, or so I thought.

Prior to submitting my application for the MA/PhD Program in Religious Studies, I was recommended by an advisor to contact A.T., a professor of Religious Studies and Chair of the committee handling Graduate-level applications for the department. I was instructed to set up a meeting with her in order to "put a face to my application." I had taken two classes with her in the past, but hadn't had any significant interactions, positive *or* negative, so I figured it couldn't hurt my chances. I did as I was told and set up the meeting via e-mail and met with her a week later.

When I walked in the door to her office, A.T. seemed friendly enough. She asked me about my aspirations and I told her that I wanted to be a writer and that I had self-published a book the year before. I didn't mention whether or not the work had been related to my studies, nor did I imply that its content was relevant to my application within the department. Upon hearing that I had a book published, A.T. turned to her computer and immediately

Googled my name; the first result was my Amazon.com page for my first book: *Disproving Christianity: Refuting the World's Most Followed Religion.*[6] I could see her computer monitor and, while I was a little bit nervous, I was sure that writing a book of compiled biblical criticisms in my spare time couldn't be used *against* me — especially because this work was completely separate from my UCSB course studies. *I was wrong.* A.T. turned to me and said, *"I need to word this carefully... you wouldn't fit in with our department's milieu because you are an atheist activist with an axe to grind."* I was stunned. I told her that the assumption was a ridiculous one, and even posed the rebuttal that a Christian who had done missionary work would certainly not be denied because of that fact — and I'd say a missionary is at least as much of an activist as I am. Sure enough, a few weeks later, my application was denied. Whether or not this interaction was the *reason* for the rejection, A.T.'s behavior was inappropriate, unprofessional, and *illegal.*

It was these words, coupled with her refusal to apologize when I confronted her in person and by e-mail, that led me to seek justice — if not within the university, then in public opinion. I wrote the article *Atheist Activist with an Axe to Grind,* and received plenty of criticism by Christians who said that, as an atheist, I shouldn't be studying religion in the first place. But, more importantly, I received numerous messages *in support* of my cause; and the article was picked up by popular atheist websites including *Friendly Atheist*[7] *and* was even mentioned by *The Washington Post.*[8]

6   David G. McAfee (2010). Disproving Christianity: Refuting the World's Most Followed Religion. CreateSpace. ISBN 1-4515-5533-4.
7   http://www.patheos.com/blogs/friendlyatheist/2011/04/30/atheist-rejected-from-grad-school-because-of-his-activism/
8   http://live.washingtonpost.com/why-do-americans-hate-atheists-herb-silverman.html

Readers wrote letters of support to the school and to the Vice Chancellor of Student Affairs for UCSB, who approached me and asked me what I hoped to gain from this. I didn't anticipate the meeting that followed, but I was happy that the people who read my story felt inspired enough to defend religious freedoms in a public sphere.

Clearly, with this incident of religious intolerance, I lost my appetite for continued enrollment with UCSB in *any* fashion, so a secondary review of my application or admission into the program would *not* suffice to make up for the discriminatory comments by A.T. And, although I maintain that the professor's actions were illegal, I did not seek to defame the campus by taking my case to trial as a result of one administrator's behavior. Instead, I asked for the one thing that could demonstrate that the Religious Studies department would *not* tolerate this type of behavior in the future and showed acknowledgement and recognition of the error. I wanted to be sure that non-religious students who enjoy studying religion would not be discriminated against in this way, so I asked for a formal letter of apology from the head of the Religious Studies department at UCSB, Jose Cabezon.

Less than a month later, thanks to the *many* letters of support[9] sent to the Religious Studies department on my behalf, and after an extensive investigation by the UCSB Office of Student Affairs, I received just such a letter. It stated the following:

---

9   http://davidgmcafee.wordpress.com/letters-of-support/

Atheist Activist with an Axe to Grind

"I am writing on behalf of the Religious Studies department to apologize for any comments that may have been made by Professor [A.T] during a conversation you had with her on November 23, 2010, about your interest in UCSB's graduate program in Religious Studies. While I was not present during that conversation, I want to assure you that it is the firm policy of the Religious Studies department not to discriminate against applicants on the basis of religious beliefs or lack thereof. If Professor [A.T] implied otherwise, then this was inappropriate. Issues of religious beliefs, activism, or activities unrelated to one's own academic work should not be considerations in the admissions process."

Now that the ordeal is over, I've decided to attend Graduate School elsewhere after taking some time to work as a journalist and publish this work. I've also since republished my first book in a revised second edition. But I am happy with the outcome of the investigation and I hope this small victory might help those non-believers who might be discriminated against based on their lack of faith. Thank you to everybody who supported me through letters to the university on my behalf. The full apology letter is available on the next page.

UNIVERSITY OF CALIFORNIA, SANTA BARBARA

BERKELEY · DAVIS · IRVINE · LOS ANGELES · MERCED · RIVERSIDE · SAN DIEGO · SAN FRANCISCO SANTA BARBARA · SANTA CRUZ

DEPARTMENT OF RELIGIOUS STUDIES
Humanities and Social Sciences Building
University of California
Santa Barbara, CA 93106-3130

Telephone: 805 893-4505
Fax: 805 893-7671
http://www.religion.ucsb.edu

May 27, 2011

Mr. David G. McAfee

███████████████
███████████

Dear Mr. McAfee:

I am writing on behalf of the Religious Studies department to apologize for any comments that
may have been made by Professor ████████ during a conversation you had with her on
November 23, 2010, about your interest in UCSB's graduate program in Religious
Studies. While I was not present during that conversation, I want to assure you that it is the firm
policy of the Religious Studies department not to discriminate against applicants on the basis of
religious beliefs or lack thereof. If Professor ████ implied otherwise, then this was
inappropriate. Issues of religious beliefs, activism, or activities unrelated to one's academic work
should not be considerations in the admissions process. If anything was said during your
conversations that gave you the impression that your personal beliefs or non-academic work
were factors in evaluating your application, please accept our sincere regrets.

I wish you a joyous commencement celebration of your achievements at UCSB and all the best
in the future.

Sincerely,

José Cabezón
Professor and Chair
Department of Religious Studies

What it Means to be an Atheist

"Atheism leaves a man to sense, to philosophy, to natural piety, to laws, to reputation; all of which may be guides to an outward moral virtue, even if religion vanished; but religious superstition dismounts all these and erects an absolute monarchy in the minds of men"
— Francis Bacon (January 22, 1561 – April 9, 1626)

As an openly non-religious individual, you will no doubt receive reactions to your lack of religiosity ranging from genuine curiosity to blind and hateful criticism. In short, you will need to be prepared to answer an onslaught of questions regarding *what* you believe, *why* you believe it, and even *if and when* you were "de-converted." In **Chapter Fourteen:** *Frequently asked Questions*, I lay out my answers to some of the questions I hear most often. But in order to answer some of these ideological questions that apply to the nature of atheism, I've put together a small description of exactly what it means to be an atheist or subscribe to a secular worldview. Oftentimes, identifying yourself as an "atheist" is harder than the rejection of the dogma itself, largely because of the negative cultural connotations as described in the *Introduction*. This chapter will help to destroy some of the common misconceptions associated with "atheist."

The most commonly asked question toward non-believers on behalf of believers, in my opinion, is regarding any ultimate "goal" or Reality present within a secular individual's mindset. "If not for God and religion, what *point* is there to it all?" they might ask. I generally respond to this type of inquiry by stating that, as an atheist, I don't claim to know an over-arching "Meaning of Life," but I *do* operate under the understanding that life should *not* be lived under the pretense that it is simply a *"test"* propagated by an invisible, intangible, Creator-God. And it should *not* be spent identifying with religious traditions and organized groups that, historically, have been at the root of a tremendous amount of oppression and violence. It is my sincere opinion that our precious time on earth should not be spent attempting to justify unbelievable acts of cruelty, death, and disease as a part of "God's Plan" or the greater good — and clinging to ancient texts that preach ill-concealed bigotry and sexism. Instead, we should find ways to make *this life* happy and satisfying, without regard to the unknowable nature of an *afterlife*. After all, as Marcus Aurelius once said:

> *"Live a good life. If there are gods and they are just, then they will not care how devout you have been, but will welcome you based on the virtues you have lived by. If there are gods, but unjust, then you should not want to worship them. If there are no gods, then you will be gone, but will have lived a noble life that will live on in the memories of your loved ones."*[10]

In the Christian tradition, according to John 14:6[11] and other biblical passages, a requirement for passage into Heaven is that you accept the Lord Jesus Christ as your savior. From this fact, a few questions immediately spring to mind:

---

10 Quote by Marcus Aurelius, Roman Emperor (26 April 121 - 17 March 180).
11 NIV 2011 John 14:6: "Jesus answered, 'I am the way and the truth and the life. No one comes to the Father except through me'."

- Would a truly fair, merciful, and just Creator really condemn those individuals who have never heard of Jesus or even those of us who have heard the name Jesus Christ, yet see no physical or historical evidence to warrant belief?

- Shouldn't someone be forgiven for simply being born into the "wrong" religion?

- Should it be enough to simply be the best person you can be? According to the Christian Gospel, the answer is simply — and firmly — "No."[12]

In addition to answering a believer's questions, it doesn't hurt to ask a few of your own that might make your stance on religion more easily understood. *"What makes you think your God is the right one?"* is an especially important question to ask any believer as it might help one realize their own cultural ties to their specific religious beliefs. In fact, there are thousands of proposed gods and goddesses with similar stories and myths that supposedly link them to reality — the Judeo-Christian God is no exception. Each religious canon has its own fallacies and contradictions that we have outgrown scientifically over time, yet the outlooks of these religions have continued to adapt and evolve with human society and morality, attempting (often without success) to discard the archaic principles within holy texts as symbolism or metaphor as the religion is handed down generation-by-generation through familial instructions. In order to prevent myself from unintentionally identifying with any of these flawed traditions, I consider myself a "naturalist" and a "rationalist" above all other *ideologies*. This means that I do not believe in any

12 2 Thessalonians 1:8

gods, devils, angels, talking snakes, ghosts, vampires, or any other supernatural beings. That does make me an atheist, but that is not how I'd identify myself foremost. I simply utilize scientific evidence and common sense to form opinions based on the best information available to me. I do this without relying on traditional and familial influences to make my decisions or encourage the invention of supernatural beings or forces in order to assign meaning or attempt to explain the unknown. Few believers acknowledge the statistical assumption that, had they been born to another family in a different culture, they would likely have had equally strong faith in another god or multiple gods... I would still be a naturalist because I've personally never seen evidence that justifies belief in anything supernatural.

Religion has been used to accomplish an enormous number of goals throughout history, both positive *and* negative. But these negative impacts remain, in my opinion, unjustifiable in the long-run: from justifying the oppression of women and lower-class citizens to being the motivation and/or catalyst for some the most brutal of wars, the mentality that one group understands a god's wishes and can act upon them, has historically been a practice of various religious traditions since their inception. It is especially true that government officials, including in the "secular" United States, adopt the idea that their "God" is somehow rooting for them, and then employ it in warfare.

Although religion has motivated violence and has long been the source of scientific restriction and regress, the origin of religious beliefs is, in almost all cases, as a crutch for providing an explanation for the otherwise inexplicable.

The "God of the Gaps" is an idea for which we, as modern humans, have little-to-no use since scientific discoveries have shown us how the earth came to be, how humanity evolved from our primitive ancestors, where the sun goes at night, and how viruses spread — leaving little room for the outdated religious explanations for these so-called "phenomena" and "miracles." In a modern paradigm, religious precepts and spirituality are adopted as a concept for the purposes of dealing with grief, fear of the unknown, and a sense of community and higher purpose. You'll find more on grief from a secular perspective in **Chapter Thirteen:** *Religion and Grief*.

All-in-all, I'm not one to dispute the therapeutic value of spirituality and I've seen religious traditions provide comfort to those who seek it out in times of great distress — however, mysticism and spirituality have never provided something that secular therapies, which don't come with the psychological baggage of religions, could not. Those people who claim to *need* religion to cope with the realities of day to day life — or to justify their morality — could not be further from the truth. In fact, for those people, a religion may provide a sense of well-being in an otherwise overwhelming world — but it rarely leads people to *solve* their problems; it often only encourages them to leave these issues up to the mystical higher-power and dodge responsibility. While this tactic may give the appearance of resolution to the believer, it is difficult to justify such an action in light of the loss of individual accomplishments and spirit. It is when the principles of religion begin to be taken too seriously at a fundamental level, to the point of extremes, that it becomes no longer therapeutic but harmful to society and the individual. This happens when men or women begin to act on God's behalf to motivate their own ambitions and priority is shifted from the important issues of the known temporal world to the faith-based belief in the next.

Being 'Good' Without God

"With or without religion, you would have good people doing good things and evil people doing evil things. But for good people to do evil things, that takes religion."
— Steven Weinberg (born May 3, 1933)

One reason that a religious person might give for having issues with your de-conversion from religion to a more naturalistic understanding of the world is that many religions propose themselves as the one unified source of an objective morality. In other words, they teach that "moral living," altruism, and general goodness are impossible without their god(s) and the Holy Scriptures that support them. According to the Christian tradition, for example, the texts assert that it is *impossible* to be moral without accepting Jesus "into your heart."[13] As an open non-believer, it will be useful to be able to explain that this is simply not the case. Not only is it *possible* to be good without God — but, I would argue, it is much easier.

The concept of a transcendent, divine, morality that is unattainable without living in accordance to a specific religion is a flawed idea for two major reasons: firstly, we can see *how* moral values could have evolved over time within society in conjunction with the evolution of other social constructs such as a sense of community, nationalism, and even democracy. Secondly, it is easily shown that *altruism* is a uniquely non-religious concept once *morality* and *worship* are distinguished from one another — as they

---

13   Most Christians would argue that *everyone* is born a sinner and will be punished as such unless the individual accepts belief in Jesus Christ.

rarely are in religious institutions. I think that what we now call *"morality"* has evolved — as nearly all social and physical human attributes have — to aid us in survival and, ultimately, reproduction. This morality requires that we be guided only by a *conscience* (or "moral sense") and not by a god or gods.

The evolution of morality can be thought about in similar terms to physical evolution. We can determine which aspects of our ancestors' behaviors best allowed for the primitive communities to flourish — therefore ensuring that those behaviors flourished in future generations and remain present (and continually changing) to this day. Variants of Charles Darwin's Theory of Evolution by Natural Selection can be used to explain many of the otherwise inexplicable traits of modern humans from mate selection to social interactions and even child rearing. What many people don't realize is that such theories can also explain the sense of morality among humans in absence of a theological (and therefore supernatural) definition.

Our understanding of what is moral is always changing. For example, until a few hundred years ago, it would have been perfectly morally acceptable to own and sell human beings as slaves. Yet today, this practice is condemned as, many would argue, *universally* immoral — of course, this does not mean that all areas of the world have adapted to this more modern viewpoint. Perhaps most importantly, the Bible still condones such behavior, and it always will. The same goes for the mistreatment of women and those individuals considered "lesser" socially — ideas that are prevalent in many religions, including and especially within Christian texts. This development, progression, and fluidity of cultural ethics and norms is precisely what makes the Bible a poor, stagnant, moral compass for today's society. Not only does the Holy Bible condone acts that our modern society would find completely unethical such as rape, murder, and slavery, but it also condemns acts like homosexual orientation in the New Testament and wearing mixed-fabric clothing and working on Sundays in the Old Testament — acts that, today, could be considered normal and completely separate from "morality." Humans are social animals by nature, much like some other primates in the animal kingdom; it is only natural that, in order to live and thrive in a society, there is some level of cooperation amongst the members of the group. This basic, evolutionary, fact is what undoubtedly led to the eventual formation of what is "moral" and what is not. If our ancestors had not realized the importance of communal cooperation, they may have become a weaker species that wouldn't have survived on a long-term timeline. In other words, if it had been *beneficial* to our primitive common ancestors to murder one's own family members, have incestuous relationships from which less capable children could be born, or act outside of societal expectations, humanity, as it exists today, may not have become a reality.

To ensure that others in the society followed the same ethical values, social contracts may have — at one time — not been enough. And promising eternal damnation or rewards in the afterlife based on behavior in this life was probably a useful way to keep people in line — in addition to the obvious benefits of dissuading revolution from the oppressed. But today, in the modern world, our values have grown and groups advocating for *religious* morality have become opposed to contemporary morality — such groups include religious extremists like the Ku Klux Klan, Jihadists, Crusaders, Nazis, and anti-abortion terrorist organizations, among others. We have in place a system, however, in which people are employed by the government to investigate, arrest, prosecute, and detain offenders based on the violation of laws that are as fluid as our cultural ideals and established by *humans*, and not humans posing as Gods — and can be amended as such. This legal system has developed over time in order to ensure one's accordance with rules and regulations that are *not* considered to be permanent or divine; this eliminates the need for a *supernatural* punishment/reward system based on an afterlife — like those often presented in ancient Holy Texts that feed on the gullibility and fear of people seeking something more than this life.

In the Christian tradition, the concept of morality is tied directly to pleasing the Judeo-Christian God; this is evident in the presence of God-serving attributes listed as the first, second, third, and fourth of the worshiped Ten Commandments present in Exodus and Deuteronomy. This means that nearly *half* of the Ten Commandments that were supposedly given directly from God to Moses to guide moral living on earth are directed toward serving God, worshiping God, and preventing "other Gods" from encroaching on "His" domain. The first four commandments don't condemn rape or slavery or bigotry — in fact, those concepts are conveniently absent from the Commandments entirely. Here are the divine, transcendent, moral goods as established in Exodus of the New King James Bible:

1. "I am the Lord your God, who brought you out of the land of Egypt, out of the house of bondage. You shall have no other gods before Me."

2. "You shall not make for yourself a carved image, or any likeness of anything that is in heaven above, or that is in the earth beneath, or that is in the water under the earth; you shall not bow down to them nor serve them. For I, the Lord your God, am a jealous God, visiting the iniquity of the fathers on the children to the third and fourth generations of those who hate Me, but showing mercy to thousands, to those who love Me and keep My Commandments."

3. "You shall not take the name of the Lord your God in vain, for the Lord will not hold him guiltless who takes His name in vain."

4. "Remember the Sabbath day, to keep it holy. Six days you shall labor and do all your work, but the seventh day is the Sabbath of the Lord your God. In it you shall do no work: you, nor your son, nor your daughter, nor your male servant, nor your female servant, nor your cattle, nor your stranger who is within your gates. For in six days the Lord made the heavens and the earth, the sea, and all that is in them, and rested the seventh day. Therefore the Lord blessed the Sabbath day and hallowed it."

5. "Honor your father and your mother, that your days may be long upon the land which the Lord your God is giving you."

6. "You shall not murder."

7. "You shall not commit adultery."

8. "You shall not steal."

9. "You shall not bear false witness against your neighbor."

10. "You shall not covet your neighbor's house; you shall not covet your neighbor's wife, nor his male servant, nor his female servant, nor his ox, nor his donkey, nor anything that is your neighbor's."[14]

In most major religions, moral living is tied to *belief*, which makes a non-believer inherently amoral from that religion's perspective. This fact makes the explanation of secular morality even more important when coming out as an atheist to friends and family. A religious person might hear that you are no longer religious and automatically associate that concept with "sin" or immoral behaviors when, in fact, true altruism is only possible *without* a theological understanding of *goodness*. Altruism is defined as a *principle of unselfish concern for the welfare of others*.[15] In other words, an altruistic action is doing 'good' for others only for the sake of the helpful act itself; this is to say that there are no ulterior motives. In this sense, not only do I think that it is possible to maintain moral standards without the crutch of religion, but I would argue that it is the *only* way to achieve true goodness and altruism. Free from the constraints of organized religion, a human being is able to express decency from one's self — as opposed to attempting to appease whatever higher power he or she may believe in. By separating *worship* and *morality*, we can act in accordance with our own human morals and are able to be less selfish in our *motivations* for kindness and moral behaviors.

14   Exodus 20:2-17 NKJV
15   http://www.merriam-webster.com/dictionary/altruism

Timing is Everything

*"Take time to deliberate; but when the time
for action arrives, stop thinking and go in"*
— Andrew Jackson (March 15, 1767-June 8, 1845)

As is the case with most important decisions in life, timing could be one of the most important factors when coming out as a non-believer to your family and friends. If *deciding* to tell your loved ones about your de-conversion is the first step, then timing the delivery is the second. Planning can prove to be very helpful in this area in that a spontaneous, off-the-cuff, announcement through an argument can catch your family off guard, leaving yourself and loved ones unprepared. When dealing with religious family members, coming out as an atheist has an even greater potential to end in rejection and pain; so, in these situations, planning an early, logical, and supportive approach to sharing your de-conversion from religion is the most important part of the process.

When it comes to *coming out*, the most simple piece of advice I can give is, "the earlier, the better." Religious family members may be upset to hear about your lack of faith in the tradition that they practice, but time will always help those who truly love you understand and accept that their religion simply doesn't reach the burden of proof necessary to warrant lifelong dedication — in the opinions of you and countless others; after all, "time heals all wounds." The time it often takes family members to understand this change is exactly why planning to express your doubts in religious institutions as early as you begin having them is such an important element in any transition to becoming openly non-religious — and making sure that your doubts are not misunderstood. It is interesting to note that, from a religious perspective, doubt and skepticism of faith is often cast as "God testing you," or "the Devil tricking you," or some variant, whereas it is much more likely that your critical thinking skills are starting to make headway.

This is not to say that the first time you question religion you should immediately tell your family that you're an atheist, but openly expressing doubt may help plant the seeds with more "traditional" family members for a future *naturalistic revelation*. What it does mean is that, if you are sure that you want to share your secularism with your family and friends, then the earlier you make the information known, the earlier they can solve their own issues with your de-conversion that stem from their own insecurities in faith-based religions and accept your choices, hopefully ensuring everyone's happiness. Disassociation with a given religious system does not *have* to be a devastating familial interaction; often, as is the case within my own family, sharing your secular mentality as early as possible can help loved ones get used to the idea and prevent major impacts in the future of your relationships. In short, as long as you take a healthy approach to sharing your de-conversion, they *will* usually get over it — it is just a matter of time.

For those who have been hiding behind an image of religiosity, timing can also refer to the literal *time* you choose to let the world know that you are no longer going to blindly follow ancient man-made scripture — that is, in relation to other familial situations and interactions. By this I mean that it is important to plan a specific — and comfortable

— time to be honest with your loved ones. As you might expect, it is usually considered bad form to "come out" in an argument about religion — and it is certainly in poor taste to purposefully belittle one's beliefs. As was discussed earlier, for some people there are therapeutic benefits for believing in something "greater" than mankind, so it is important not to judge them for their beliefs — just as it is important for them not to judge you based on your lack of faith in deities. This type of confrontational behavior will ensure that your message is delivered to family in a time of stress or tension and will subsequently convey those negative feelings; in most cases, that only serves to make the acceptance process more difficult for you and your family in the long run. When you finally decide to show your skepticism toward your religious tradition, it is also important to remember that your religious friends and family members have probably held these belief systems for *many* years and they were most likely engrained in them as young children — you cannot expect them to suddenly *realize the error of their ways* and give up on religious mythology without significant thought and self-discovery. These are beliefs that have been flourishing and fortifying in some cases since childhood and today may provide comfort for those who fear the unknown or even retain a fear of purposelessness in a more general sense, and they will not be easily shaken. Nor is it your responsibility to de-convert them; instead, think of it as your obligation to present your opinions in a logical manner, educate loved ones on your motives for separating from religion *if prompted*, and love your family no matter what they choose to believe in or disregard; after all, it is a person's *actions* that define them — and not their belief system or lack thereof.

The act of being honest with those for whom you care deeply regarding your thoughts and opinions on "divine" matters should be a celebratory one. The sheer will-power it takes to break away from the cultural constructs that were (in many cases) enforced in your psyche as a child is impressive in itself, and risking familial pain and disappointment in the spirit of truth and transparency is even more commendable. Support is what you need more than ever, but some believers who care for you might see this *transitional* period as one of confusion and "sin" — one that they are sometimes ill-equipped to handle. It is often the case that, in these instances, a de-conversion is met with anger and sadness as a result of instinctual and reactive behavior on behalf of the loved ones who once showed nothing but respect and admiration. This is not because religion makes people inherently bad or corrupt, it seems more likely the case that they are simply *set in their ways*, and without the support system necessary to deal with such a shock to the cultural norms to which they have grown accustomed. Just as you need the support of your family to know that you won't be disowned for disputing theistic claims, your family may need support to know what this means for them and their faith. Having a concerned and religious loved one talk to a religious leader *might* help console them — depending on what that leader chooses to represent to them — but most often it helps to involve other family members who are supportive or otherwise able to help mediate the interaction between yourself and your more fundamentally religious kin. In **Chapter Sixteen**: *Resources & Support*, I will provide a helpful directory of organizations and communities that provide much needed support for former believers and their family members.

For those parents who did everything in their power to ensure the realization of a pious and God-fearing child, finding out that he or she is *non-religious* can be a shock to the system. This, however, is no excuse to keep your lack of faith a secret from your loved ones; dishonesty does not *build* personal relationships. In fact, hiding the truth often aids in the destruction of these relationships. And letting them know that you *do* love them — and therefore your honesty with them is of the utmost importance to you — can be an easy way to break the tension between you and your theistic relatives. The planning of the event itself can be liberating on its own, not to mention the confidence one gains from a successful "revelation" after which your ultimate goal is realized, the support and validation of your loved ones for simply being *you* — without prejudices or discrimination based on belief or lack of belief. It is not uncommon that the fact that one has gone through so much trouble to share one's dismissal of faith with their loved ones in a supportive and organized manner actually *demonstrates* to loved ones how important their familial opinions actually *are* — this sometimes spurs the beginning stages of the acceptance process on its own, and the power of this concept should not be underestimated.

Confrontation

*"A man is accepted into a church
for what he believes and he is
turned out for what he knows."*
— Samuel Clemens (November 30, 1835 - April 21, 1910)

Confrontation is a natural part of any interaction involving a member of a family dissenting from the others, especially when it comes to the topic of religion or politics. But, on a more fundamental level, confrontation results from these religious discussions for one simple reason: *You're telling them that their most fundamental beliefs are wrong.*

In many cases, religious beliefs are firmly held ideas that have been reinforced since a *very* young age. When you tell someone — even if it is a family member or close friend — that you don't *believe* in their God, a defensive reaction isn't surprising. Oftentimes, you're telling them that everything they've ever known, everything their parents and their childhood idols ever told them, is *wrong.* For some non-believers who used to be active within a religious institution, this point is well understood. Letting go of these principles can be one of the hardest things to do, so having a loved one who previously agreed with you holding the opposite position can be jarring. But that doesn't necessarily mean that every situation needs to be handled with "kid gloves," it simply means that one must take into account the amount of indoctrination that has often occurred in a given individual.

Even if you aren't intending to set out persuading people to give up their religions, even if you couldn't care less what other people believe, when you say, "I don't believe in god(s)," it will always mean that, if they do, you believe they are *wrong*. This fact is one aspect that separates religious identification with other disagreements and discussions common within families. And it is about a topic that some people hold closer than all else — religion. In fact, that is one of the distinguishing features that separates "coming out" as an atheist and coming out in the traditional sense as within the LGBT community. It is not as if saying, "I'm gay," inherently means, "Straight people are *wrong* to be straight."

That's part of why coming out as an atheist is so confrontational and one of the main reasons that many people who disbelieve choose to simply remain silent about the issue. Unfortunately, taking that route doesn't progress tolerance toward a secular mindset or educate the believer about secularism, nor does it make it easier for future atheists to be open about their beliefs without fear of reprisal. In fact, an atheist who remains completely silent and/or complies with religious norms out of cultural familiarity may actually make coming out more difficult for others by playing into the assumption that everyone is a theist and increasingly separating people of no religion from the public view.

If there *is* a familial confrontation as a result of your coming out, it is important to recognize that if your position is by definition opposed to theirs, then the opposite is also true. Just because their position may be more popular (in most regions of the world, including and especially the United States), it does not make it any more reasonable or obvious — in fact, it is quite the opposite. After all, as was discussed in *Author's Note: Born Atheist,* without cultural indoctrination, all of us would be atheists or, more specifically, while many may dream up their own Gods as did our ancestors, they would certainly not be "Christian" or "Jewish" or "Muslim" or any other established religion. That's because, without the texts and churches and familial instruction, there are no independent evidences that any specific religion is true. Outside of the Bible, how would one hear of Jesus? The same goes for every established religion.

Misunderstandings about atheism also contribute to the "controversial" aspects of coming out. It is not uncommon that a religious person sees your disbelief in their particular Creator as an affront to said Creator. I can't count the number of times I've been accused of "hating God" for simply not believing in any deities — a rather contradictory concept if you think about it. But that does not stop some people from taking another person's atheism as a personal attack on their ideas and their God. This type of cultural stigma is common and can generally be counteracted by education on the basics, starting with the definition of atheist as discussed in the Introduction: *a lack of a belief in a god or gods.*

As an "out" and vocal atheist, I've gotten used to hearing religious objections that result from conflicts between believers and non-believers… one of the most common from Christians is the claim the "Jesus still loves you." While there are often good intentions behind this phrase, for a non-believer, it doesn't provide the comfort that it may for a Christian. I, for one, honestly care more about the love here on earth than the possibility of being "loved" by an unprovable and unknowable being. I'm more concerned with the love I share with my family and close friends... it is love that doesn't come with the price of faith and rejection of their love doesn't result in eternal damnation.

"I'll pray for you" is another popular phrase uttered by religious people in interactions with non-believers. While some no doubt have positive intentions, this is usually seen as a condescending remark. If a believer really thinks their god will alter its divine plan to satisfy his or her requests, I like to suggest that they focus all of those prayers on the sick and the dying, and leave me out of them.

Confrontation is a natural part of the coming out experience and in many interactions. And dealing with confrontation is something that people get used to in the context of a family. It may help, however, to make it known that you aren't seeking to *change* the way they think, but instead that you should have the same freedom from religion that most modern governments guarantee their citizens. The fact that, as an open atheist, you are telling believers they're *wrong* does not necessarily mean that it is a bad thing. In a modern context, being able to voice your opinions and challenge those of the majority is critical. It is these challenges from non-religious people all over the world that cause believers to give a second thought to the archaic traditions that they identify with and, in many cases, also ignore. If a situation arises in which the conflict is out of control, it is always best to seek professional guidance in the form of therapy and/or counseling. In *Chapter Twelve: Extreme Situations*, you'll find information about how to find secular therapists.

Be Prepared

To "hope for the best and prepare for the worst" is helpful advice when approaching such a divisive topic; after all, you don't *know* how your loved ones will react — so be prepared for some unwelcomed responses. With the negative connotations that the religious majority has historically bestowed upon secularists and non-religious individuals (an idea that, unfortunately, continues to be taught in modern churches), there could be a knee-jerk reaction on behalf of your loved ones to respond negatively toward your lack of belief. In Christianity, this can be traced back to hateful scripture such as 2 John 1:9-11: "Anyone who runs ahead and does not continue in the teaching of Christ does not have God; whoever continues in the teaching has both the Father and the Son. If anyone comes to you and does not bring this teaching, do not take them into your house or welcome them. Anyone who welcomes them shares in their wicked work." Other passages, such as 2 Chronicles 15:12-13, actually condone putting atheists to death for their beliefs.[16] Some of the more closed-minded and fundamental believers may even associate your secularism with devil-worship or "Satanism." I should not have to point out the ridiculousness of this connection.

---

16   2 Chronicles 15:12-13: "They entered into a covenant to seek the Lord, the God of their ancestors, with all their heart and soul. All who would not seek the Lord, the God of Israel, were to be put to death, whether small or great, man or woman."

Part of the planning process of making your skepticism public knowledge might involve ensuring that you have prepared rational arguments that respond to what issues your family and closest friends may or may not bring up during this interaction. For those "active atheists" or atheist activists who generally believe that religion is a negative force in the modern landscape, it is considered common practice to engage in all-out rational debate regarding the existence of god(s) in anonymous interactions with the religious; in this particular case, however, it may be easier to begin by simply adopting a "to each their own" mentality in which you lovingly accept each other's dogmatic preferences unconditionally. This is not to say, however, that you should not provide *reasons* for your de-conversion; it simply means that early on, the best approach may be mildly describing *why* you have chosen *reason* over *faith*. Over time, it is even possible that you might convince your loved ones that they don't *need* religious doctrines to live happy and full lives, perhaps freeing them from centuries-old supernatural dogmas, too.

Preparation for coming out as an atheist includes choosing wisely how and with whom you begin the process of public de-conversion. Some relatives and close friends might be more understanding than others; it is advisable to seek these people out for starters. You may want to "test the waters" in this regard by casually bringing up the topic of God and/or religion to those people closest to you whose religious preferences are unknown to you or you imagine might be sympathetic to your cause. It is not the case that all believers will condemn you; there are many open-minded believers who will not see your atheism as inherently bad or offensive. Sometimes, you will be surprised to find that people you have known your entire life and assumed to be religious are, in fact, skeptics or unconcerned with "divine" matters altogether; this can be a welcoming initial interaction for those who might be scared of judgmental reactions and stressed personal relationships with fundamentalists in the family. There is only one way to find out if some of your loved ones feel the same way as you do and *you* could, in fact, be providing *them* with the support they need, too.

Just as religion is (ideally) considered to be a *personal* matter,[17] it might help to pose your secularism as a similar entity to any fundamentalist family members from whom you fear negative reactions or rejection. In other words, you may want to phrase your atheism in a way that warrants little to no discussion in order to avoid further interrogations or "sermons." An example of this could be, "I don't want religion to be my *motivation* for behaving in a moral manner, I believe in the goodness of humanity, I have *faith* in nature," etc. These types of vague statements discourage further inquiry while retaining a sense of openness and honesty regarding your beliefs surrounding the presence of deities. Being prepared with these types of remarks may aid you in dealing with more closed-minded individuals, who otherwise might seek to re-convert you into their religion; this — I should reiterate — can be a very tedious and dissatisfying argument for both parties.

---

17   Matthew 6:1-4: "Be careful not to practice your righteousness in front of others to be seen by them. If you do, you will have no reward from your Father in heaven. So when you give to the needy, do not announce it with trumpets, as the hypocrites do in the synagogues and on the streets, to be honored by others. Truly I tell you, they have received their reward in full. But when you give to the needy, do not let your left hand know what your right hand is doing, so that your giving may be in secret. Then your Father, who sees what is done in secret, will reward you."

How can you really *prepare* for coming out as an atheist to religious kin? Just like anything else, preparation is aided by *practice*. We already discussed the option (when available) to contact a less-religious, maybe distant, relative or acquaintance who might be more understanding of your secularism, but what about those of us who do not have the luxury of being acquainted with such an individual? This is where online forums, blogs, and chat rooms become useful. All over the internet there exist websites specifically dedicated to the discussion of religion, atheism, religious tolerance, and rational free thought. These community-based programs and clubs will be more fully outlined in **Chapter Fifteen:** *Resources & Support*, where I will include a directory of helpful blogs and informational websites. Interaction with other skeptics and believers with whom you aren't acquainted on a personal level will help you to be vocal about your secularism without worrying about consequences in your daily life; it is also important, however, to not carry over any disrespectful or begrudging tones from these anonymous interactions into your conversations with those you love and for whom you care — in this instance, it is often simpler to show as much love and respect as possible in the engagement, if for no other reason than to show that your secularism hasn't affected any sense of "morals" or "proper behavior" that they saw in you in the past, for this is a common misconception among religious people being presented with secularism for the first time in a personal and formal dynamic.

Coming Out to Your Significant Other

"We are told that people stay in love because of chemistry, or because they remain intrigued with each other, because of many kindnesses, because of luck. But part of it has got to be forgiveness and gratefulness."
— Ellen Goodman (born April 11, 1941)

Coming out as a non-believer to a fundamentalist or otherwise religious spouse is one of the most difficult situations involving de-conversion. It is easy to see how a marriage or partnership might suffer from such a divisive distinction being revealed between the two partners. But on the other hand, what can be more crucial in such an important relationship than being honest and sincere with one another? Above all else, it is important to remember that this *can* be a survivable interaction, even if your partner is fervently dedicated to a specific tradition, if it is approached in a manner in which the concerns of both individuals are properly addressed. By introducing your secularism to your spouse in a calm and understanding manner, you can ensure a smooth interaction as long as you make it abundantly clear to your partner that this difference in faith *will not* affect the terms of your established relationship.

The *True Love Argument*, which addresses love and the Christian concept of "Heaven," might help you convey to your partner why the ideas of True Love and the Christian doctrine are truly incompatible. I will excerpt this complex yet concise argument from a prior five-step description of it in my first book, *Disproving Christianity and other Secular Writings:*[18]

1. Heaven, as described by the Christian tradition, is eternal happiness in communion with God.

2. True love consists of a relationship in which neither party can be truly happy without the other.

3. Two people in a relationship of this nature could, because of different beliefs, be separated in the afterlife, and one could be sent to heaven, without his or her significant other.

4. The Christian in heaven could not be happy without his or her partner, thus causing heaven to become a place of everlasting pain and sadness.

5. Because heaven is described as eternal happiness, this creates a contradiction in which the concept of a Christian heaven fails to be viable.

6. Therefore Christianity, which presupposes eternal bliss in heaven postmortem, cannot be the true Word of an all-knowing God.

Coming out as a non-believer to your spouse or significant other becomes increasingly crucial when the possibility of interaction with *children* comes into play. Whether you have children already or plan to in the future, the question will inevitably rise regarding how you and your partner will raise the children in terms of religious ideologies. Your partner may want to share the wonders of his or her religious tradition with the child while it is just as likely that you, likely having experienced and rejected this type

---

18   David G. McAfee (2011). Disproving Christianity and Other Secular Writings (2nd edition, revised), pp. 31-32. Dangerous Little Books. ISBN 0-9564276-8-5.

of religious indoctrination, might hope to prevent this behavior. It may be the case that neither partner can convince the other to change ideological positions on the issue and, in that instance, there are cases in which each parent presents their ideas surrounding religion and spirituality as the time arises, without unity. While this is not *ideal*, it may be better than compromising what you truly believe in order to satisfy your partner's desires to teach children that a specific tradition is "the right one." A healthier compromise in the decision of *how* to introduce religion to your children (if at all), would be one in which the parents work collaboratively to teach about *various* religious traditions and scientific positions simultaneously, letting the child decide for him or herself whether or not to adopt a spiritual or naturalistic understanding of the universe. It is important to note that more serious interactions — like the scenario described above — may warrant professional guidance or counseling.

Whether or not children come into play when making the decision to come out as a non-believer to your significant other, it is one of the most difficult decisions that you may have to face throughout your journey to becoming a public non-believer. The importance of this decision, however, does *not* translate into the importance of the difference itself: highlighting the similarities in mentality between yourself and your partner, as opposed to the differences, will help him or her in understanding exactly how *little* religious differences matter in the big picture. Discussing how your *moral* compass has remained untainted, for example, might assist in shifting the conversation from religious *differences* to ideological *similarities*. For examples of secular morality, refer back to **Chapter Five:** *Being 'Good' Without*

God. To further shed light on the topic of religion, atheism, and relationships, I'll excerpt from Nickolas Johnson's testimonial, which is fully published in *Chapter Eleven: Testimonials*. Nickolas is an atheist and secular humanist who is married to a Christian:

> "… A year or so later I met another girl. A Christian girl. **After a few years of dating, we married in her church (her choice) in July 2007.** In the first year of our marriage, I began reading more non-fiction books. I started with "Why People Believe Weird Things," and then was hooked on free thought-style books. A few months after we married, my wife fell and greatly injured her back. The next few years were especially difficult for the two of us. The injury caused her to have two surgeries and I had to leave my job to stay at home to take care of her. **Throughout all of this, I'm sure many people probably would expect some sort of shift in faith from one or both of us, but our opinions remained intact. Her religious faith seemed unscathed and my atheism only grew more fervent with the more knowledge I gained.** I never questioned or blamed God because it seemed futile, and I think she must have found some sort of peace with her views.
>
> **My wife and I have been married for nearly five years now and I think religion plays a bigger role in my life than it does in hers.** I like to read books regarding biblical historicity and logical arguments while she goes to her old

church back where her mother lives whenever she's in the area. **Sometimes my opinions of her religion may seem reflective of her but I'm not brash because of some sort of disdain for that part of her personality; more so I have an open, honest relationship with her and nothing is too taboo to talk about.** Her views on religion have always been what I would call "Diet Christian," but I suppose everyone else just refers to as liberal; that has allowed us to discuss things without getting into any irrational arguments. **When it all boils down to it, if you share the same core values and put importance in the same values it really isn't that hard to be with some one that disagrees with you on other things.** There are certain things she is passionate about that I do not much care for and vice versa, so we never have any reason to argue over those things. **There are also certain things, like prayer, that we may not agree on but it is not something we bother arguing over.** She has a very open mind and is going to two free thought conferences with me this year.

If I had to give any advice to someone who has opposing opinions of a loved one in regards to religion it would be this: stay calm, try to keep an open mind, don't interrupt, and never lose sight of why you're talking with the person in the first place."

Coming-out to Your Significant Other

Establishing a New Sense of Community

"Indeed, organizing atheists has been compared to herding cats, because they tend to think independently and will not conform to authority. But a good first step would be to build up a critical mass of those willing to 'come out,' thereby encouraging others to do so. Even if they can't be herded, cats in sufficient numbers can make a lot of noise and they cannot be ignored."
— **Richard Dawkins,** *The God Delusion*

From weekly church services and gatherings to summer camps and holiday events, a religion often fosters a sense of community for its followers. Many people who transition out of a religion and were previously involved in the social aspects of their religious traditions find this to be one of the most difficult parts about leaving the faith. In these cases, it is not uncommon for a church to have provided most of one's sense of community — and losing that can be a big deal.

In some fundamentalist and rural religious communities, the church provides the vast majority of social interactions in a person's life. An individual might be born into a family in which everything — from education to extra-curricular activities — is governed or sponsored by a particular church. In these cases, leaving the religion can be more difficult than simply "coming out." Many times, these individuals are forced to give up everything they've ever known if they make the courageous step to leave their religion. This is especially true in certain sects of the Church of

Jesus Christ of Latter-day Saints — or Mormon — religion, which is itself a denomination of Christianity founded in the 1820s as a form of Christian primitivism. In these situations, a dramatic relocation is sometimes necessary.

For those whose entire lives may not revolve around religion — but that a new sense of community would be helpful after losing the church community — there are quite a few options. For starters, some sites like www. Meetup.com provide a platform for groups to schedule and organize secular events. Like religious organizations, some of these groups plan weekly gatherings and/ or discussion groups — but they aren't limited to "atheist" topics. Some meetings are centered on a holiday, and others simply provide an event for non-theists to attend with likeminded people — examples include barbeques, book clubs, pool parties, etc. In *Chapter Sixteen: Resources & Support*, I will list a directory of helpful organizations that work to provide community interaction specifically for atheists and agnostics.

Having likeminded friends and social acquaintances is important, especially when a non-believer's current friends and family are not supportive of his or her religious stance. As is the case in all instances of discrimination or social tension, talking and sharing ideas with people who face similar issues is a helpful therapeutic tool. Talking openly about your non-belief with non-judgmental people you already know is obviously ideal, but for many, that's not an option.

If you, as is the case with many who make the transition out of a religion, feel as though it takes away from your practiced holiday celebrations, there are plenty of non-religious options for holiday celebrations, too. Websites like *www.secularseasons.org* list Humanist celebrations and events focused on the separation of church and state, free thought, and rational thought. Others, like me, choose to celebrate the common holiday traditions and simply separate the religious component.

For many, developing a new sense of community takes place online. There are thousands of secular websites and groups on larger platforms dedicated to atheist dating and networking, and can provide a safe haven for discussion about separation of church and state, religious criticisms, and other secular issues. There are also numerous groups, pages, and communities on Facebook — as well as other major social networks. In Chapter **Sixteen:** *Resources & Support*, I'll include a sampling of the larger atheist-themed online networks.

For children, "Church Camps" are all too common. These camps provide children opportunities to socialize and learn important skills, but are also extremely useful tools for indoctrination. Many camps have some sort of religious agenda, but there are options for those of us who don't wish to send our children to a camp where they might be told *what* to believe. **Camp Quest**, an Ohio-based "summer camp beyond belief," provides an educational adventure shaped by fun, friends, free thought, science, and humanist values.[19] The camp offers a mix of traditional summer camp activities and educational activities related

19 http://www.campquest.org

to the Camp Quest mission. If you're an atheist parent, you should also note *www.atheistparents.org*, which hosts parenting resources including articles, forums, a blog, and related links.

For those secularists who miss the larger church gatherings, there are numerous conventions, conferences, and rallies that are dedicated to sharing the message of free thought and skepticism. Here are just a few:

- **The Amaz!ng Meeting**: The Amaz!ng Meeting (TAM) is an annual celebration of science, skepticism and critical thinking. People from all over the world come to TAM each year to share learning, laughs, and the skeptical perspective with their fellow skeptics and a host of distinguished guest speakers and panelists.[20]

- **American Humanist Association Annual Conference**: The American Humanist Association (AHA) is an educational organization in the United States that advances Humanism, a progressive philosophy of life that, without theism or other supernatural beliefs, affirms the ability and responsibility of human beings to lead personal lives of ethical fulfillment that aspire to the greater good of humanity. AHA was founded in 1941 and currently provides legal assistance to defend the constitutional rights of secular and religious minorities, actively lobbies Congress on church-state separation and progressive issues, and maintains a grassroots network of 150 local affiliates and chapters that engage in social activism, philosophical discussion and community-building events.[21]

20 http://www.amazingmeeting.com
21 http://www.conference.americanhumanist.org

- **Committee for Skeptical Inquiry Convention (CSICon):** CSICon is dedicated to scientific inquiry and critical thinking. The conference is produced by the Committee for Skeptical Inquiry in collaboration with Skeptical Inquirer Magazine and the Center for Inquiry.[22]

- **Freedom from Religion Foundation Annual National Convention:** The Freedom from Religion Foundation (FFRF) promotes the constitutional principle of separation of state and church and educates the public on matters relating to non-theism. Incorporated in 1978 in Wisconsin, the Foundation is a national membership association of more than 17,000 freethinkers: atheists, agnostics and skeptics of any pedigree. The Foundation is a nonprofit, tax-exempt, educational organization under Internal Revenue Code 501(c) (3). All dues and contributions are deductible for income tax purposes.[23]

- **Global Atheist Convention:** The Global Atheist Convention is an annual secular gathering based in Melbourne, Australia. The event is sponsored by the The Atheist Foundation of Australia Inc., which began in South Australia in 1970 when the members of the Rationalist Association of South Australia decided that a name change would proclaim their basic philosophy, which began in Greece 2500 years ago.[24]

- **Reason Rally:** The Reason Rally is a movement-wide event sponsored by the country's major secular organizations. The intent is to unify, energize, and embolden

22 http://www.centerforinquiry.net/about/committee_for_skeptical_inquiry
23 http://www.ffrf.org/outreach/convention
24 http://www.atheistconvention.org.au

secular people nationwide, while dispelling the negative opinions held by so much of American society.[25]

- **Skepticon**: Skepticon is an annual skeptics convention set in Springfield, Missouri. Springfield is home to the Assemblies of God and several religious universities (such as Evangel and Drury). The area is affectionately referred to by many locals as the buckle of the Bible Belt. In Fall 2008, JT Eberhard, Lauren Lane, and the MSU Chapter of the Church of the Flying Spaghetti Monster invited PZ Myers and Richard Carrier to the Missouri State campus to criticize belief in god. The event was well-attended and was retroactively dubbed Skepticon.[26]

This is only a small sampling of some of the larger atheist/agnostic conferences and conventions. There are a growing number of similar events each year and, depending on your area, there may be numerous local events, too.

In addition to the various educational events and conferences listed above and the Internet groups mentioned earlier, there are many localized organizations dedicated to secularism and/or humanism. There are comprehensive lists of such meeting groups at *www.atheists.meetup.com* and *www.infidels.org/org/local.html*; other websites also serve as great resources for identifying these local groups. If you are a student or interested in affiliating yourself with secular groups on college or high school campuses, Secular Student Alliance has compiled a Campus Group List available here: *www.secularstudents.org/affiliates*.

25 http://www.reasonrally.org
26 http://www.skepticon.org

Testimonials

*"There is no greater agony than bearing
an untold story inside you."*
— Maya Angelou, (born April 4, 1928)

In the **Author's Note:** *Born Atheist,* I told my story of "de-conversion" from my first doubts in the Christian dogma that my family attempted to instill in me as a child, to my decision to study religion at UC Santa Barbara and begin writing about secular issues. I feel that, by sharing this story, readers gain a more complete view of my perspective on religion and can perhaps even *learn* from my successful "coming out." I never considered myself a "Christian," but I still faced some pushback from some of the more fundamentalist Christians in my family. Although, in my case, I wasn't threatened with excessive familial retribution, I *did* experience discrimination for my lack of belief when applying for a Master's Program for Religious Studies at University of California, Santa Barbara; that incident was more thoroughly discussed in **Chapter Three:** *Atheist Activist with an Axe to Grind.*

In order to give readers a broader range of the issues they may face when becoming openly atheist — and therefore increase the likelihood of identification with similar scenarios or experiences— I sought out six atheists to share their stories as part of this book. Each story is unique and represents the true experiences of one man or woman. Although each testimonial will share the common thread of a transition into a secular lifestyle, they will also be unique in that the authors span the racial, political, and geographical spectrums. It is my hope that these stories *will help give* insight to the large percentage of atheists who, for fear of rejection or misunderstanding, have not been open about their lack of faith. In some cases, the people featured in this chapter will have been ostracized or rejected by fundamentalist peers. And, in some, they have been met — as should always be the case — with love and respect.

To begin, I'll post an excerpt from my own coming out story, which is wholly available in the *Author's Note: Born Atheist*:

> "I don't remember a particular time in my life in which I believed in the validity of a particular religious tradition, but eventually even I had to break the news to my family and become "open" regarding my secular mindset. My parents were not always religious people... they may have abused substances religiously — but, when I was very young, church was probably the last thing on their minds. When I was two years old, my parents divorced and began their separate lives pursuing drugs to feed their addictions; thankfully, my grandmother volunteered to care for me until my mother or father could afford (financially and emotionally) to raise me. She never mistreated me or abused me, but she was the first person in my life to introduce me to religion and the authority of the Christian church. My grandparents with whom I spent the majority of my childhood considered themselves Fundamentalist Baptist Christians — and I was raised in a way that, they thought, would encourage similar ideologies in me.

When I was a bit older — around six years old — I went to a Christian church with my grandparents; this was my first real experience with a religious institution. The church, located in a small town in Northern California, considered itself "non-denominational," and the service usually consisted of a pastor reciting well-chosen biblical passages for about an hour and providing some minor inspirational interpretations. Needless to say, I was not moved by the experience — and didn't take the idea of church seriously. Even though this doctrine was being force-fed to me for as long as I can remember, I always had questions about its veracity — questions that, I quickly learned, were considered inappropriate to ask. My grandmother was a self-described traditional, god-fearing, Christian woman — it wasn't until much later that I would realize the closed-mindedness that this mindset bred in her and others..."

Jason Sciple
Location: Texas (Kingwood)
Age: 33

Jason lives in the Bible Belt. A wanderer of religions, he was eventually led to abstinence from it altogether — but not before he studied to become a pastor. As is often the case, once Jason learned more about his religion, he became more and more skeptical about its veracity. Jason struggled with his disbelief at first, as many do, still clinging to the archaic principles with which he was raised.

> *"I found myself just referring to myself as non-religious for a while as I was scared to use the 'A-word,'"* *Jason said. "I now proudly accept my atheism and am passionate about speaking up for secularism, free thought, reason, science, and logic."*

My name is Jason, and I'm an atheist. This feels weird to write for a guy that grew up in Southeast Texas and once was a worship leader studying to be in the ministry. After an upbringing in Catholicism, I left at age 17 and spent time in Methodist, Assembly of God, Vineyard, and Non-Denominational congregations. I took courses at a bible school with the hope that one day I would become a pastor. As a result of some questions about my beliefs in one of my final courses on bible doctrine, I ended up choosing a different career path. For the next 15 years or so my faith started peeling away. I didn't realize what was happening, but I was gradually losing many core beliefs of the Christian religion. *Was there really going to be a "Second Coming"? Were my homosexual friends really going to burn in an eternal lake of fire? What about my friends of other faiths?*

Was Jesus really the Son of God? Was he born of a Virgin? Was he the only way to salvation?

These questions tormented me and led me to study the origins of Christianity and how the bible was put together. I became suspicious as I noticed things like the time lapses in the writing, contradicting books, questionable authenticity of the authorship of certain books, and the different forms the bible had taken over the years as the church continued to disagree over which books were inspired. I also noticed things in the bible I had somehow missed before. When I chose to read the bible without the filter that it was the infallible word of God, I started seeing some terribly atrocious things that God was responsible for: genocide, killing of women and children, killing non-believers, killing homosexuals, etc. When I considered these things combined with the idea of eternal torment for people who merely didn't share my faith, it no longer logically fit with the idea of a loving and compassionate God. Through these studies I came to the conclusion that Christianity was a myth not all that different from many religions all throughout history. Toward the end of this journey, I was attending a very liberal Episcopal church that allowed me the space to have my questions. One friend, in particular, supported me through my doubts and encouraged me in my seeking. However, it was a Sunday morning while standing to recite the Nicene Creed that something hit me. **I began the prayer, "We believe in one God..." I had to stop. I just listened as I realized I no longer believed.**

When I first acknowledged that I wasn't a Christian, I still felt like something else must be out there. I still clung to a vague concept of God and described it as the sacredness at the center of our lives. I started studying the Eastern philosophies of Buddhism and Taoism. I didn't want a new religion, but I enjoyed some of the philosophical teachings of Buddha and Lao Tzu. I still felt as if there was a God, but perhaps he/she/it would meet you through whatever tradition you chose. I started writing about these thoughts and questions in a public blog. I started to receive emails and phone calls from concerned friends. I was told of the slippery slope I was on and how they would be praying for me. My friends were clearly worried about me. After a couple of months, I learned that some of my family had been reading my blog and were equally worried. I moved the blog to an anonymous location and reached out to different online communities for support. **I began to feel very alone with one exception, my wife, Julia**. She had started seriously doubting the faith about a year earlier, but had remained quiet about it. I was lucky to have her by my side as I struggled through this. She and I became closer than we had ever been as we started to feel like we had no one else besides one another and our two young sons.

In a reaction to the loneliness, I wondered if I had made a mistake. I studied more, contemplated, and even *prayed*. However, through the continued struggle my beliefs were further reinforced and I realized that I no longer just wasn't a Christian, but I was an *atheist*. Though I was open to evidence that suggested otherwise, as far as I could tell, there was no God. It took a while for me to get comfortable referring to myself as an atheist. In fact, I often avoided the subject. **There was such a stigma associated with that label and I knew that if my mere questioning of my faith and studying Eastern philosophy was worrisome to my friends and family, atheism would certainly devastate them.**

Regarding my friendships, I was mostly right. Since many of our relationships were with friends we met through churches, we lost what we had in common. There were very few instances where people just quit talking to us strictly because they couldn't stand to be friends with atheists, but rather we weren't the people they knew before. We were the ones that changed. Without casting blame, we just drifted apart after we ran out of things to talk about. Though we maintained a few relationships, many are now non-existent or forever changed.

Aside from the strained friendships, **family would prove to be tough.** I love my family and we've always been relatively close to each other. While they all belong to different denominations in the Christian faith, they all participate at some level. Things felt weird for a while and there was unspoken tension on many occasions while we all struggled with our emotions. On my side of the struggle, I was feeling like a victim and as if everyone was disappointed in me. On their side, **I think they hated to see me leave something that had been so dear to them.** My mom talked to me about how hard it was for her and my dad to read my blog. They wished they knew what they could do to help me. **She also told me they wondered what they had done wrong.** This particular thought hurt since I considered myself a decent person. I have a good career, a beautiful family, and have never been in any kind of trouble. I simply no longer subscribed to the faith of my childhood. I know this wasn't meant to hurt me, and I understood how hard it must have been for my parents to see this. Their Catholic faith is a part of who they are and has always been something they have strongly identified with. While everyone was generally pretty cordial with me, I knew some of my family was struggling with it. The tension I felt made me want to stay to myself and the loneliness persisted. My online community of friends and blog readers wasn't really enough to make up for the losses I felt.

As I approached the anniversary of my departure from faith, I finally started to find comfort. **The main way I found this was in coming out.** I have a couple of close gay friends to whom I talked through this struggle and one pointed out that what I was feeling was really similar to how he felt when he was trying to come out as a gay man. *You just want it to be okay to be yourself. You want so badly to say how you feel about things and just want people to allow you the freedom to feel that way. This coming out process for me has been progressive.* It was easy online where you can always find someone who agrees with you, but it is been much harder in person living in Kingwood, Texas. In this part of the world, you don't run into many atheists in your day-to-day life. I found myself just referring to myself as non-religious for a while as **I was scared to use the "A-word."** I now proudly accept my atheism and am passionate about speaking up for secularism, free thought, reason, science, and logic. I've developed a passion for helping believers and non-believers alike to value secularism and equality. **Every relationship is different, but with most relationships it is just becoming old news.** I even have a friend who jokingly refers to me as his atheist friend and likes to remind me that I'm the only atheist he knows. There are some I can talk with freely and others where we just avoid the subject. **Either way, our social life is mending, and I owe that to coming out and finding comfort in just being myself. I'm finding that as I get more comfortable with myself, others start to accept this as part of who I am.**

Julia Sciple
Location: Texas (Kingwood)
Age: 32

Julia grew up in a very religious home. Her overly-religious upbringing led to fear and guilt as a child, a common occurrence in homes prone to fanatical religious beliefs. Although she questioned her religion at a young age, she has been a Christian most of her life. In fact, when she finally shed her religious belief, she was forced to break the news to her husband, who was a Christian.

"Accepting these feelings and expressing them to my husband wasn't easy," Julia said. "Church had always been a part of our life. He was a former worship leader and Bible School student."

My parents met each other while both attending a small Bible College in Houston, Texas. My father, a New Yorker raised in a Catholic Church, had a "born again" experience while serving in the Marine Corps. Once discharged from the military, he decided to attend the small Houston bible college with the hope of becoming a missionary in Africa. My mother is from Arkansas and was raised in a Pentecostal Church. She left home at the age of 18 to attend the school. They married two years after meeting one another at the college. **Needless to say, I grew up in a very religious home.** I don't recall a Sunday morning or a Wednesday evening that we weren't in a church service or bible study. **At the age of five, I accepted Jesus into my heart and was "saved."** To this day I can still remember showing them the heart that I made in Sunday School that said, "I asked Jesus into my heart today." **To my parents,**

following Jesus was what we lived for and was something that was never to be doubted.

At a very young age, I remember having questions about the Christian faith. One specific question I remember asking my father was, "As Christians, how do we know that we're right?" I think I questioned this because I had neighbors and classmates that were from different denominations. **I also couldn't understand why a loving God would only reveal himself to certain people while much of the world wouldn't know him.** As a child I remember my heart aching for them. **I couldn't understand why we were so special to have the revealed truth while others didn't.**

Growing up in a very religious home and having parents that were fanatical Christians, there were many discussions of Heaven and Hell. **I was taught that people who didn't accept Jesus into their heart weren't "saved" and would go to Hell when they died.** I was also told that I could go to Hell if I didn't ask for Jesus to forgive me of my sins on a daily basis. **Unfortunately, this caused a tremendous amount of fear and guilt.** While I wasn't a perfect child, the fear of dying and going to Hell led me to be a well-behaved child until my teen years. As do most teens, I went through a little rebellious stage. **This is when my guilty conscience started to affect me almost daily.** I had visions of what Hell looked like and how I would suffer there because I didn't always make the right choices. This was painful for me. **I don't think I will ever understand why my parents thought that it was okay to let their children suffer in this way.** I have three other siblings that also dealt with this and still *believe* this to this day. I am a mother of two small children and I have a baby on the way. I can't even imagine making my precious children suffer in this way. I'm completely aware that my children will hear about God, but I'll stand up and protect them from ever being tormented with threats of eternal damnation. My oldest son, who is at the time of writing nearly six years old, has asked many questions about God. **Family members and classmates have talked to him about God.** My husband and I have explained to him that we don't believe in God, but that many people do. **We've explained that he'll understand this more as he grows older.** He says that he doesn't believe in God and compares Him to the Easter Bunny, Tooth Fairy, and Santa Claus.

For the first thirty years of my life, I was a Christian and believed that Jesus was the only answer. I attended church and longed for a deep connection with God. **On many occasions, I would pray and ask God to reveal himself to me.** I wanted to see miracles and have personal experiences with God. **While there were times I thought I may be experiencing God, I often wondered why I didn't experience Him like others did.** I wondered if I just wasn't good enough. **I later started to question if God was even real.** I wanted to believe that some of the good things that happened in my life were the result of God being present, but I often wondered if giving God the credit was just what I was taught to do when something good happened, and that it really didn't have anything to do with him at all. I wondered why everything had to be accredited to God. These questions started to haunt me. At first it was difficult to accept that I was questioning God's existence. It went against everything that I was taught and left me having more fears. **I dealt with these thoughts for nearly a year before I was vocal about it.**

Accepting these feelings and expressing them to my husband wasn't easy. Church had always been a part of our life. **He was a former worship leader and Bible School student.** At the time I started seriously doubting, we had adopted a much more liberal faith and were attending an Episcopal Church. **I found myself not wanting to participate because of my doubts.** When I first brought up these things to my husband, it was difficult. At that point he and I weren't on the same page. **He still believed and found it difficult to consider questioning his faith.** Most Christians believe that when two people marry, they become one, and I feared that this could possibly tear us apart. **He worried about what we would teach our kids.** We continued to attend church and I became more vocal about it for several months. **My husband started to research how the Bible was formed and, along the way, discovered that he may have questions after all.** After much study, we finally came to the realization that it wasn't crazy of us to question things. **My last prayer to God was just over two years ago.** I decided on that night that if I didn't get answers and hear God's voice, I was no longer going to live as a Christian. **It goes without saying that I didn't get answers.** I'm almost 33 years old and I'm now an atheist. I've never felt so *free*. I'm free from the guilt that once tormented me. I'm free from the thoughts of Hell. I no longer believe in God. My life no longer revolves around this imaginary creator that lives in the sky. **I believe that life is too precious to live in constant fear that there is a higher being that controls what happens to us when we die.**

While this new outlook on life has brought me much liberation, it wasn't without its share of pain. **Coming out as an atheist had social ramifications that I underestimated.** Given my family's religious background, this didn't sit well with them and created some tension that still exists today in some respects. **I know they feel like I'm just lost and I'm afraid they'll never understand how I feel about these things.** They'll never understand the liberation that I feel as an atheist. **Our friendships also suffered and we're still in the process of rebuilding our social lives.** Living a suburban life in Texas hasn't made it easy, but we're trying. **No matter what, I'm happy to say that my husband and I now live godless lives and enjoy what each day has to bring.**

Hugh Kramer
Location: Los Angeles, CA
Age: 59
www.examiner.com/atheism-in-los-angeles/hugh-kramer

Hugh Kramer has had a fascinating religious history. From Jewish beginnings, to a "transformation" in college, he has seen various views along the religious spectrum. Now Mr. Kramer is an atheist blogger in Los Angeles. He said the horrific events of 9/11 impacted his religious identification.

> *"So I became an agnostic. I remained one for decades," he said. "It took the events of 9/11/2001 to change that."*

Some people experience epiphanies; something occurs, perhaps even something ordinary and in an instant, **their previous worldview shatters and they are changed forever**. I envy those people for my progress to new ways of seeing the world has always been plodding and often painful. **My personal transformation from theist to atheist took place over more years than many of my readers have been alive.** I never intended to become an atheist and in some respects I was only dragged into atheism kicking and screaming. Experience and what Martin Luther, the father of Protestantism, called *"Die verfluchte Huhre, Vernunft"* (**That damned whore, Reason**) are what dragged me there.

I did have some small advantages though. **I grew up in Los Angeles**, which is not a particularly religious town and was raised in a not-particularly religious Jewish family. **We took the existence of God for a given** and observed a few of the major holidays but otherwise the only strongly-stressed Jewish rule we were taught was to live life as good people. By the time my parents decided I needed to learn more about Judaism in preparation for my Bar Mitzvah (the Jewish coming of age ceremony), I was too old (11 going on 12) for the transplant to take. **I still believed in God and still considered myself Jewish, but I couldn't take all the dietary and other restrictions seriously.**

The next transformation didn't take place until I got to college. There I discovered science and philosophy. Oddly enough, it wasn't the works of greats like Hume or Locke or Nietzsche that had the biggest influence on me. It was something I read before them that made me receptive to new mental landscapes like theirs. I'm almost ashamed to admit that it was an otherwise stupid piece of nonsense called "The Crack in the Cosmic Egg" I was assigned to read in Sociology 101. It was mostly New Age woo (unscientific, non-evidence-based assertions), but the central concept, that there was more than one way to see the world (what German philosophers call "*Weltanschauung*") struck me almost with the force of a revelation. **I feel stupid admitting it now, but the idea had just never occurred to me before**. As this new thought gradually sunk in, it had the effect of opening me up to new ideas and concepts. **I was still vaguely theistic, though, because I wanted to believe in a *fair* universe; that there was some kind of balance between good and bad or right and wrong.**

That idea started teetering because of another book, *Beyond Freedom and Dignity* by behavioral psychologist, B.F. Skinner. The book argued that free will was an illusion and that belief in individual autonomy was hindering both the scientific understanding of psychology and the development of a healthier, happier society. While I found those ideas convincing at the time, what I took away from the book more permanently was an under-standing that **the evidence-based scientific method was probably the best tool mankind has ever developed for the accurate evaluation and acquisition of knowl-edge**; and because it provided techniques to compensate for personal bias, I decided it could be applied to per-sonal knowledge as well. I re-examined a lot of beliefs at this time that I had taken for granted. Some held up under scrutiny. Some didn't. **I changed my stance on the Vietnam War, for instance.** More importantly, I took another look at my ideas about religion and found them wanting. **There was no good evidence of a balance in the universe between what I thought good or bad. There was no good evidence of any force personally inter-ested in it or me either.** I couldn't prove there wasn't *some* kind of supernatural force behind the universe but I also couldn't see that the claims of special knowledge of any religion had more than faith going for them either.

So I became an agnostic. I remained one for decades. It took the events of 9/11/2001 to change that. I can't remem-ber a time when I didn't think religious fanatics were nuts (so nuts in fact, that I coined the word **"fanutic"** to describe them). It just hadn't been brought home to me before on such a personal level how *dangerous* to the modern world religion could be.

And it wasn't just Islamic fundamentalists that scared me. I began to notice how religion also provided cover for extremists in America and in my own community. **I saw them attacking civil rights for women and homosexuals.**

I saw them trying to undermine science in the classroom and in scientific research. I saw them infiltrating the military, the judiciary and school boards, all in an effort to roll back the clock to a time when human rights were dispensed at the whim of divine autocrats (or at least their self-styled interpreters) if at all. I could not prove there were no gods, but it had been a long time since I believed in any. I called myself an agnostic, though, because I'd felt no pressing need to make any declarations about it.

Now I did.

I still can't prove there are no gods, but I think them highly unlikely and don't believe in any. More than that, I think the belief in such supernatural overlords is, in essence, an embrace of the irrational and dangerously skews a person's perspective even in its milder forms. In its more virulent forms, I think it is a malignancy that eats individual freedom and threatens the existence of a civilized world.

That's why I became an atheist.

And an activist.

Elizabeth Rouse
Location: England
Age: 23

Elizabeth Rouse didn't grow up in a very religious home. "Saved" at around 10 years old, Elizabeth said that surrounding herself with other Christians helped suppress the questions she'd had since childhood. As is so often the case, research and a passion for science led to her non-belief. Being surrounded with Christian friends, her decision was not easy.

> *"I was met with a lot of anger and frustration," Rouse said. "They had no interest in what I had to say and just immediately started to talk me out of it. When I said I didn't want to be convinced otherwise, they wanted nothing to do with me."*

When I was a child, there was no god in my house. We didn't go to church or have family prayers. My mother was very young and I don't think she had time for god. It wasn't until I was 10 that I was introduced to the church community. My aunt's father-in-law was the pastor of a Baptist church and she suddenly became very passionate about the Word of God. My aunt started having conversations with me that I never thought about, like, **"Where did man come from?"** and, **"What happens when we die?"** I all of a sudden had so many questions that I *needed* answers for. So, every Sunday she would take me to church. I made a lot of friends and became saved. As I grew older I didn't go to church as often but that was just because I was becoming a lazy teenager, and not because I didn't believe.

My first boyfriend was very religious; in fact, our first date was at a church event. **Surrounding myself with Christians helped stifle my need for more answers.** Being around my aunt and my boyfriend's family made me think if these answers are good enough for them then obviously they must be true, and if I have more questions, then all I need is faith. **It was at this point at the age of 14 that the cracks in my beliefs started to show.**

At the start of my freshman year of high school, I had a lot of friends and seemed happy on the outside. **However inside, doubt started eating away at me.** The Church's answers were becoming less and less satisfying for my growing mind. **More and more questions were going unanswered.** I started doing research on my own and I found that many of the scientists I was starting to admire where atheists. Sadly, as my love for philosophy and science grew, I could feel the distance grow between me and everyone I was close to. All our conversations seemed silly and childish. **After I worked up enough of a defense to support my new belief, I decided it was time to tell my friends about it.** I didn't think it would be too bad, I mean they were my friends after all. I knew there would be a lot of questions, which was more what I was preparing myself for. I was very mistaken. **I was met with a lot of anger and frustration.** They had no interest in what I had to say and just immediately started to talk me out of it. **When I said I didn't want to be convinced otherwise, they wanted nothing to do with me.**

Only halfway through my first year of high school, I had to start over. **Being from a very religious community, it wasn't easy.** I was no longer afraid to be myself and for the first time the world made sense to me. But it took me a while to find friends that understood that, even if they didn't agree with it. **I was the topic for a lot of prayer groups and I was well known throughout the school.** I was no longer shy about my thoughts or feelings and I wanted others to know that. I was in the principal's office a few times (once for wearing a homemade Darwin shirt, and another because I wouldn't stand for the pledge of allegiance). **I was never afraid to argue my case and I never received punishment.**

I am now almost 24 years old and happily married to my high school sweetheart. We have two beautiful children and I'm hoping that my story inspires them to be themselves, and know that no matter what struggles you are faced with all you need to get through it is to belief in yourself! Looking back, I'm proud of myself for sticking to my guns and not letting anyone make me feel inferior.

Cleta Darnell
Location: Texas (Dallas area)
Age: 56
http://contributor.yahoo.com/user/424223/cleta.html

Cleta Darnell was raised in a Southern Baptist family. She said her family's negative actions — namely in their attempts to keep her from straying from religion — helped push her toward non-belief. Baptized, as many are, before she truly knew what the process meant, Darnell started out as a "questioner" before formerly proclaiming her atheism. She said she was treated very differently after becoming open about her non-belief.

> *"In my experience, being honest meant being ostracized and shouted down — most of all by my family,"* she said. *"I did get a few licks in, though."*

I know a lot of people who have been "converted" to one religion or another. I, on the other hand, was raised in a solidly Southern Baptist family and, for want of a better word, eventually *de-converted* from Baptist to atheist. Far from preventing me from straying from religion as they hoped, my family's ideas, actions, and attitudes made me less of a believer over the years. **I have always believed that the only reason most of them ever did the "right" thing is out of fear of otherworldly reprisals.**

My earliest memories of going to church are of crying when I didn't get to go to Sunday school. I now know that it was the *social aspect that attracted me,* even though I was often treated badly or ignored by my classmates. Their families had moved up, financially, faster than mine and I was often ostracized for not dressing as well as the others. I now realize that an undiagnosed hearing loss, which left me clueless to the nuances of things around me, also contributed to my lack of conformity.

In an attempt to fit in, **I was baptized around age 10 or 12**. I knew even then that *I didn't really mean it*. I only vaguely remember deciding to be baptized. My recollection of it may be hazy, but I know that I did it mostly out of peer pressure. I was still something of an outsider among the kids in both my school and my church (many of whom were the same people) and I somehow thought being baptized would bring me more acceptance. Despite my need for acceptance, the process left me feeling like a charlatan. **The whole thing went against my logical side.** Long before the whole "intelligent design" movement, I asked several people including my parents and my Sunday school teacher, who was also one of my teachers in public school, if it wasn't possible that there was a compromise between evolution and Creationism. **My inquiries were met with a resounding, "No!"** That rejection of any possibility of free thought opened my mind to the possibility of being free of my family's delusions. Now don't get me wrong, I didn't go straight from wannabe believer to atheist with no steps in between. *I started out as a questioner.*

My initial salvation from religion began when I was a teenager in the form of my best friend's free thinking family. Although she and I drifted apart many years ago, I still think of the good they did for me. In fact, I still think of her mother very fondly and visit her on occasion. If it weren't for that family, I don't know what I might have done when my mother, who was the center of my world, died when I was barely 15. Everyone in my family except my father had spouses and children to rally around them and **Daddy, well, he had his**

church — the same church I already felt out of step with. My friend's family served as my anchor when I felt everyone and everything else had set me adrift. Without their support, I believe I would have gone into a serious downward spiral.

The other thing my friend's family gave me was permission to question, to wonder if what I had learned was based in fact. Questions that were met by my family and church with *"No,"* and *"Don't question, just believe,"* were met with discussion and encouragement when posed to her family. With them I was exposed to other religions, specifically Catholicism, which was their family's "official" religion. With them, I attended masses in both Latin and Spanish. The Latin I knew nothing of and the Spanish I knew a little of, but they explained things as they went along, or after the fact when appropriate. Prior to this, my only exposure to "other" churches was attending my sister's wedding in a Methodist church and a couple of visits to the fundamentalist Baptist church my niece attended. They were so strictly fundamentalist that I was asked to leave a skating party I attended with my niece because **I wasn't wearing nice enough clothes, specifically a "Sunday school" dress.**

In my experience, being honest meant being ostracized and shouted down — most of all by my family. I did get a few licks in, though. As a rebellious teenager left alone with a detached father, I learned how to lash out when I wanted attention. It was not uncommon for me to threaten to date a black or Hispanic boy or, worse yet, a CATHOLIC! **My favorite jab at Daddy, though, was to refer to the bible, his beloved bible, as a book of Jewish fairy tales**. That one statement could cause a full relief map of the state of Texas to appear in the veins on Daddy's forehead.

Daddy never did give up on his religion. One day, Mere weeks before his death at age 94, he asked me what I was reading. I told him and he thumped, literally thumped, his bible and said, "This is the only thing I need to read." Because of his age, and my refusal to mar his last days with dissent, I neither laughed at him nor answered with what I thought. Later that day, I vented by updating my Facebook status with, *"If you never read anything other than what you already believe, how do you know that what you believe is true?"*

As an adult, I tried never to begrudge Daddy his religion. Before he died, I made a nice hand-stitched cover for his old bible. I fear it gave my family false hope of my impending "salvation," but I would have done the same no matter what book it was. I also helped arrange for him to be buried with his bible. It was his companion in life so I felt it was only right that it accompany him in the casket. My main reason for this was to minimize the potential for fights and bad feelings among several of his grandchildren who had already expressed an interest in having the bible. Putting the bible in his casket with him took it out of play. When the man from the mortuary asked if we didn't want to keep it, I told him that too many people wanted it and this was a way of preventing family squabbles. I refrained from telling him I felt it was **just so many pages of fiction and there are plenty more copies of it to go around.**

Daddy wasn't the only religious zealot in our family. My oldest sister, more than 15 years older than me, can hold her own as a religious fanatic. Once, when my son was acting up, as children will do, she told me to put the heel of my hand on his forehead and tell the devil to *"be gone!"* Now bear in mind that this woman has one son who has been in prison since his late teens for murder, and her oldest son has almost completed his life's work of drinking himself to death. Looks like that plan really worked for *her*; and still, **she has the gall to wonder why I don't believe.**

Her daughter is my favorite family bible-thumper despite the fact that for quite some time **she was a member of a Christian sect that I considered to be a true cult**, where the pastor often used the pulpit to rail at her parishioners for a variety of personal transgressions because, after all, anyone and anything she didn't like was *"evil."* My niece and sister, among other family members, now know my opinions about religion, but at least **my niece has finally learned that she will never be able to change my ideas and attitudes, so she accepts them.** That doesn't stop her from occasionally trying, but she has learned to gracefully accept "shut up" as an answer. I wish her mother would do the same. She loves to make little jabs at me whenever possible. Her most recent attempt involved quite pointedly discussing with her daughter, in front of me, how *"When we go to heaven, God will make us forget friends and family members who weren't saved so we won't be unhappy."*

It is no surprise to me that I hedged about my (non) religious views for years. It is only with the advent of the atheist groups online, which I found through a nephew who also happens to be an atheist (thank you, Donald)[27] that I have become more open about my views. **Many people who matter very much to me still disagree with my views, some quite vocally so. Nevertheless, I find that feeling free to express my thoughts and feelings about religion to be liberating.**

---

27 http://contributor.yahoo.com/user/111823/donald_pennington.html

Nickolas Johnson
Location: O'Fallon, Missouri
Age: 27

Nickolas Johnson tried Christianity and, like many of us, the more knowledge he accumulated, the stronger his sense of rationality grew, and secularism quickly followed. Nickolas writes from a very unique perspective in that he's married to a Christian woman.

> *"My wife and I have been married for nearly five years now and I think religion plays a bigger role in my life than it does in hers," Nickolas said. "I like to read books regarding biblical historicity and logical arguments while she goes to her old church back where her mother lives whenever she is in the area."*

I believe that my journey into the realm of disbelief began when I was young. As a child, my mother instilled a sense of fairness in me that has stuck around to this day and is one of the driving forces behind why I do not believe in any gods and why being a good person has always taken precedence over any sort of belief system.

It began when I was about 10 years old. We lived in a small community of about 200 people in rural Missouri that had two or three churches, one of which I attended from time to time. I can still remember the long services, which I dreaded out of the overwhelming sense of boredom, followed by an arts and crafts-type Sunday school that I rather enjoyed. My participation in the church was eventually followed by my willful attendance to church camp. **I honestly can't recall what I did outside of sitting around listening to boring old stories and swimming the**

first year, but I can tell you with extreme clarity how my second year ended.

The end of the second year at church camp was a big bonfire where they put aside time for all of the children to give themselves to the lord and accept Jesus Christ into their hearts. **Never mind how confusing saying "accepting so-and-so into your heart" sounds to a pre-teen, I still never understood why it was required and why there was such a big fuss about it.** The children all gathered and then we prayed. Slowly, one by one, the kids all began crying. Then I, out of fear and empathy, began to cry as well. The adults of the camp came around consoling us telling us things like, "It is OK. You are SAVED now!" and, "Let him into your heart." **But the only thing I could think about is how horrifying it was to see a bunch of my peers crying about seemingly nothing.**

After that year, I decided that faith was not for me. **I never rebelled against my parents, stole, did drugs, drank, or did anything illegal**. I never seemed any more lost than the next confused teenager and Lucifer didn't make me his puppet like all of the teachings said. From time to time I did wonder if I was missing out, but it seemed like **every time I looked back at religion, all of its hypocrisy creepily glared back at me**.

I didn't really encounter religion again until I was in my first serious relationship. We were both non-believers for a good portion of the relationship and never really worked well together as a couple. In short, we fought all the time. **At some point our boss told us his story about when he found faith and how it made him a better person, so we decided to journey into the realm of faith to see if**

it would salvage our relationship. She jumped in both feet first and I trod softly in the shallow end hoping that it would help her curb her rage and jealously issues. At first it seemed to work. She was more calm and willing to listen to me and I was glad to be listened to for once. **But as with all the other things that helped her some, it eventually gave out.** She began lashing out at me and I realized that not only did I not want to live a façade, but I did not want to be with her any longer. **After this realization, it was easy to not go back to the church that had failed to do even a simple thing in the eyes of its master.**

A year or so later I met another girl. A Christian girl. **After a few years of dating, we married in her church (her choice) in July 2007.** In the first year of our marriage, I began reading more non-fiction books. I started with "Why People Believe Weird Things," and then was hooked on free thought-style books. A few months after we married, my wife fell and greatly injured her back. The next few years were especially difficult for the two of us. The injury caused her to have two surgeries and I had to leave my job to stay at home to take care of her. **Throughout all of this, I'm sure many people probably would expect some sort of shift in faith from the both of us, but our opinions remained intact. Her religious faith seemed unscathed and my atheism only grew more fervent with the more knowledge I gained.** I never questioned or blamed God because it seemed futile, and I think she must have found some sort of peace with her views.

My wife and I have been married for nearly five years now and I think religion plays a bigger role in my life than it does in hers. I like to read books regarding biblical historicity and logical arguments while she goes to her old church back where her mother lives whenever she is in the area. **Sometimes my opinions of her religion may seem reflective of her but I'm not brash because of some sort of disdain for that part of her personality; more so I have an open, honest relationship with her and nothing is too taboo to talk about.** Her views on religion have always been what I would call "Diet Christian," but I suppose everyone else just refers to as liberal; and that has allowed us to discuss things without getting into any irrational arguments. **When it all boils down to it, if you share the same core values and put importance in the same values it really isn't that hard to be with some one that disagrees with you on other things.** There are certain things she is passionate about that I do not much care for and vice versa, so we never have any reason to argue over those things. **There are also certain things, like prayer, that we may not agree on but it is not something we bother arguing over.** She has a very open mind and is going to two free thought conferences with me this year.

If I had to give any advice to someone who has opposing opinions of a loved one in regards to religion it would be this: stay calm, try to keep an open mind, don't interrupt, and never lose sight of why you're talking with the person in the first place.

Extreme Situations

"In extreme situations, the entire universe becomes our foe; at such critical times, unity of mind and technique is essential – do not let your heart waver!"
— Morihei Ueshiba, (December 14, 1883 – April 26, 1969)

In some regions, being an atheist — or even professing a religion different from those that the government sanctions — is not only a crime, but a crime that is punishable by death. And, contrary to popular belief, blasphemy laws still exist in some parts of the world, and they are often strictly enforced. There are very few instances in which remaining silent about your non-belief is a good idea — but there are exceptions to every rule.

In February 2012, an atheist in Indonesia was jailed for nothing more than a comment on Facebook in which he said he did not believe in God, according to *Al Jazeera,* an independent broadcaster owned by the state of Qatar.[28]

Although Indonesia is officially a "secular" nation, every citizen has to have a religion and register himself according to one of the official five religions — as recognized by the government.

This instance is just one of many across the globe and, especially in highly religious areas in the Middle East, speaking out against the state religion is considered blasphemy and it is not uncommon to see the death penalty imposed

---

28 http://www.huffingtonpost.com/2012/01/20/atheist-attacked-faces-jail-time-facebook-god_n_1219778.html

for such actions. In the United Kingdom, the death *penalty* for *blasphemy* was only abolished in 1676.[29]

In Iran and some other constitutional Islamic theocracies, the law against blasphemy is derived from *Sharia Law*, the moral code and religious law of Islam. Blasphemers are usually charged with "spreading corruption on earth," or *mofsed-e-filarz*, which can also be applied to criminal or political crimes. The law against blasphemy complements laws against criticizing the Islamic regime, insulting Islam, and publishing materials that deviate from Islamic standards.[30]

These laws are commonplace in fundamentally Islamic nations — in fact, in May 2012, Kuwait's parliament approved a law that calls for the death penalty for insulting the Muslim Prophet Muhammad or his wives and relatives. In an era in which you'd expect scientific progress to impede the emergence of violent religious fundamentalism, it is sad to see that, in some areas of the world, the tide is turning in the opposite direction.

My point in describing these violent and discriminatory acts against atheists around the world is not to dissuade anyone from being open about their lack of supernatural belief — instead it is to illuminate the negative force of many religions against non-believers, even in modern times. If you feel that your life will be endangered by being vocal about your atheism, I would certainly not recommend doing so — but, perhaps, it may be time to relocate to an area in which that danger is absent.

29 The Ecclesiastical Jurisdiction Act 1677 (29 Car.2 c.9)
30 "Annual Report of the United States Commission on International Religious Freedom May 2009."

If you are located in an area in which you won't be jailed or otherwise legally punished for your lack of belief — but fear more intimate and emotional reprisals — it may be a good idea to seek professional counseling in the form of therapy or psychological treatment. This can be very helpful for those individuals interested in coming out, as well as those who have already faced discrimination from loved ones and hope to talk to someone about the issues religion has caused in his or her life.

It is important, though, that the therapist you choose isn't going to reinforce the negative stigma of non-theism or otherwise try to *reconvert* you — there are many "doctors" who are affiliated with a particular religion and see their sole responsibility as reconversion, as opposed to helping the struggling individual with their problems. To help provide a network of secular therapists, Darrel W. Ray, author of *The God Virus* and founder of Recovering from Religion, founded the Secular Therapist Project. Here's an excerpt from the group's website describing what that organization is all about:

> *"There are many secular people in your community that have mental health needs. Unfortunately, many secularists report that they cannot find a secular counselor in their community. We know there are often many secular therapists, but they cannot openly advertise as secular for fear of losing clients or other negative social and professional consequences. By registering you increase the likelihood that secular clients will find you and they will be able to avoid therapists who allow their religious, spiritual or supernatural beliefs to inform their therapeutic approach."*31

31 http://www.seculartherapy.org

The Secular Therapist Project is a unique answer to a common problem, and there are other similar secular projects being formed every day. And with an increasing number of atheists coming out across the world, we should expect this trend to continue. After all, the only way that these new non-religious services can arise is if an entrepreneur sees a sufficient need.

Religion and Grief

"You want a physicist to speak at your funeral. You want the physicist to talk to your grieving family about the conservation of energy, so they will understand that your energy has not died... You can hope your family will examine the evidence and satisfy themselves that the science is sound and that they'll be comforted to know your energy's still around. According to the laws of the conservation of energy, not a bit of you is gone; you're just less orderly."[32]
— Aaron Freeman, (born June 8, 1956)

One of the therapeutic benefits of spirituality is the hope that the idea of an afterlife sometimes instills in those experiencing grief from a loss. If you lose a loved one, and you truly believe that you'll see that person again in Heaven, the argument can be made that the religious person's mentality provides a sort of peace with the loss. However, this can also work in reverse.

Regardless of your religious beliefs, you should never tell a mourning mother that it was "God's plan." For some people, that can be worse than saying nothing at all. For a non-believer, the words that are meant to console a religious person can do quite the opposite. A mother who loses her son, for example, might not wish to hear that God took her child or that she might see him as an "angel" someday — she probably just wants her son back. At very best, this type of language is irrelevant and not applicable

---

32 This is an excerpt from a longer quote by Aaron Freeman, American journalist, stand-up comedian, author, cartoonist, and blogger.

to atheists or anybody who doesn't subscribe to that particular worldview.

Holly Samel was 19 years old when she found out she was pregnant. She was excited about the pregnancy and was already a couple of months along. She and her husband went to the hospital for an ultrasound — it was a boy. But, she said, the ultrasound technologist was acting suspiciously.

"She kept measuring stuff over and over," Holly said. "I was in there for more than an hour and she said he was moving around too much — I asked her what was wrong, but it wasn't her job to tell me."

Holly and her husband left the ultrasound without being told any specifics, but they were happy. She began to call everyone she knew to tell them that her unborn child was a boy. Just as she was hanging up the phone after giving her mother the good news, her excitement quickly turned to immeasurable sorrow. Holly got the call from her midwife.

"She told me he wasn't going to make it. I started crying instantly," Holly said. "I have never felt anything that fast or real before. Even in my most uncontrolled emotional moment, I did not lean on religion. I had been non-religious my whole life. It never even crossed my mind that it could help me out." Holly later found out that her son had a rare form of dwarfism that meant his bones were improperly developed, coupled with other genetic defects — he wouldn't survive. Holly was five months pregnant at the time.

"They offered me an abortion because there was absolutely no chance of him making it, but I chose to continue the pregnancy," Holly said. "My midwife allowed me to come in and listen to his heartbeat as often as I wanted. I wanted to keep what I had with him as long as I could. The stress put me into early labor anyway when I was almost six months along, and Ethan weighed 1.9lbs. Looking back at how tiny and frail he was, plus the religious sympathies getting to me, I started to think about what they could possibly think Heaven would be like for him. I kept wondering who would care for him, or if they feel he wouldn't need care in Heaven. They all wanted to tell me how sure they were he was now in Heaven having a good afterlife, but no one had the details about it that I craved."

Since that time, people told Holly many things about her experience — especially the typical "comforting" statements: "He's in a better place now," or "It was part of God's plan," or that God (for whatever reason) "needed Ethan."

Although she wasn't religious, she just ignored the statements at first. She knew they meant well. That stayed true until a few years later, when her own grandmother said something that Holly couldn't ignore.

"She found out I was an atheist and e-mailed me. She said she knew that I had to believe in Heaven because I want to see my son again. She said my atheism was just a phase," Holly recalled. "She had the same thing happen to her first son. I couldn't help but think that it has been more than 40 years since she lost her son and everyday she's needed to believe she is going to see him in Heaven. It has been only five years since I lost Ethan, and I never needed a similar comfort on my worst days. I feel like atheism or a non-religious grieving process allows you to deal with the death more honestly."

Holly wanted to learn more about how and why this happened to her son.

"I asked the midwife to explain to me as best she can," Holly said. "I was confused and I didn't believe that he really had no chance. They told me the science behind why he couldn't have lived, and about how horrible his life would have been if he had."

If anything, the experience reinforced her atheism. She knew that no all-loving and all-powerful God would allow this type of injustice — not just for her, but for the millions in similar situations around the world.

In the end, what really helped Holly were logical explanations of her son's genetic disabilities, and not the false hope that religion offers. Holly said, with the complexities of religious portrayals of afterlife, assuming a pre-birth child is in Heaven, there's no telling whether or not that would even be a good thing. Would he be a fetus in Heaven? Would he grow? Who would care for him? Would he go to Hell? She said none of it made sense — and scientific explanations and reason helped her through the grief.

For those non-believers experiencing the death of a loved one, there is no more prominent support group than Grief Beyond Belief. Grief Beyond Belief is an online support network for people grieving the death of a child, parent, partner, or other loved one — without belief in a higher power or any form of afterlife. Atheists, agnostics, humanists, freethinkers and anyone else living without religious beliefs are invited to participate. Grief Beyond Belief was launched by Rebecca Hensler after the death of her three-month-old son.[33]

33 https://www.facebook.com/faithfreegriefsupport

Frequently Asked Questions

*"Who questions much, shall learn
much, and retain much."*
— Francis Bacon (January 22, 1561 – April 9, 1626)

In this chapter, I will lay out some of the questions I'm asked most often as a secular advocate — along with a brief response for each one. The answers are my own, and do not necessarily apply to every non-believer. But they do give a look into my worldview, most specifically that of an atheist and naturalist. As an atheist coming out, you will no doubt encounter some of these same questions... my hope is that my responses will help provide some insights into your own answers as well as more clearly understand my motivations and intentions.

Q: I know you don't believe in the Christian God, but do you believe in other gods or the devil?

A: I don't believe in any supernatural or paranormal beings, forces, or entities simply because there is no evidence for their existence. I also don't believe in magic, superstition, or astrology. I would, however, be open to changing my mind — for the right evidence.

Q: Do you *know* there is no God?

A: No, I don't claim absolute certainty on the non-existence of gods... but uncertainty should never be enough to warrant belief. Nobody knows absolutely how we got here, but I'm more comfortable with following the scientific evidence on the subject than I am in proclaiming the existence of a deity or deities out of my own ignorance of the facts. Depending on how you define "god," the existence of one ranges from highly improbable and unnecessary to nearly impossible — but, if you define God as the prayer-answering deity of the Abrahamic religions that interferes with earthly affairs, it is fairly easy to conclude that it likely does not exist. If there is a deity, it is completely detached. It has used methods of creation that are indistinguishable from nature, it has declined to make itself known for all of recorded history, it doesn't interfere with earthly matters, and has made itself impossible to observe. There is no evidence for such a being and its existence is improbable and unnecessary at best, but even if you believe in that God... why would you think it would want to be worshiped?

Q: Why did you decide to become an atheist?

A: I never "decided" to become an atheist — and, in fact, I don't think belief or non-belief is something you necessarily choose. In my case, I simply followed the evidence. The question presupposes that theism or religiosity is the natural state, which it is not. We are all born free from all religious affiliations and only come to believe in such things after being introduced to it — so, atheism is the default position. Although some children are not indoctrinated with a specific religion before the age of reason, there are many more who are — I was lucky in that my religious upbringing didn't stick. I never believed in gods or goddesses because I've never seen evidence to support such claims. For me, everything has always been explainable in natural terms, so assigning a deity or deities to anything seemed counter-productive, especially when the attributes of the deity aren't even agreed upon by its own followers — and believers use their god to justify what they think is right and to condemn what they think is wrong. Because the existence of deities is both highly improbable and unnecessary, taking the leap of faith to believe in one simply never occurred to me.

Q: There is a God-shaped void in your heart. Don't you feel that your life is missing something without God?

A: If such a God exists, there must be a glitch in its system... I'm very happy. I do what I love, I have an amazing family, I do good for others when I can, and I'm not hindered in the least bit by not believing in deities. There is no void. In fact, I'm quite happy that I don't fear death. An eternity of anything could eventually be torture, and I'm happy to live my life to its fullest without regard to the possibility of a second.

Q: What would it take to change your mind?

A: The only thing that would change my mind is concrete evidence. If there were substantial testable, peer-reviewed, evidence that showed that the presence of a deity was highly probable or required for anything on earth, I'd certainly be subject to reevaluating my position. But that will never happen because of the very nature of all deities — and all things supernatural; at the end of the day, a believer has to rely on "faith." If in some radical miracle, the Abrahamic God revealed his existence to the world, I'd accept the belief in the deity — but I still wouldn't worship it. The jealous and angry God that justified the killings of millions, sent plagues upon first borns, and abhorred homosexuals would not be worthy of my worship.

Q: Why do you dislike believers and/or religion?

A: I don't dislike believers. The average believer, while arguably gullible, is guilty of nothing more than wishful thinking. I don't even dislike religions... they can be very interesting from a phenomenological and historical approach. But when religion justifies violence, impedes scientific progress, and gives motivation to strip people of human rights, I feel that criticism is warranted and necessary. But my critiques shouldn't be confused with disdain; pointing out the negative aspects of religion and inconsistencies within belief systems does not equate to hatred or persecution.

Q: Why don't you believe just in case we are right? What do you have to lose? [*If you gain, you gain all. If you lose, you lose nothing. Wager then, without hesitation, that He exists. – Pascal's Wager*]

A: I can't simply will myself to believe, belief doesn't work that way. I don't believe in gods not because I don't want to, but because all the evidence points to the contrary — and I don't accept things on "faith." Belief without evidence just doesn't compute for me. So, I suppose I could pretend to believe, but do you think that feigned belief resulting from a fear of "Hell" would make one worthy of "Heaven" to an all-knowing God? Salvation usually requires genuine acceptance of a deity, and that's something I cannot give for any radical claim without substantial supporting evidence. Even if I were to genuinely accept a deity, though, which religion is the "right" one? From Bahá'í to Buddhism to Wicca to Zoroastrianism, hundreds of religions with thousands of denominations exist globally today and countless others have been cast aside over time, many of them claiming authority over the next. Accepting one God on faith would condemn me to all others — so, skepticism of all deities is the more prudent approach.

Q: You just don't understand religion because you have never felt God. Have you ever had a personal relationship with your Creator?

A: No, I've never been a believer. In fact, I've spent most of my life trying to figure out why people believe what they do. But, I'm an exception to the much more common path to atheism; many non-believers (perhaps most in certain regions of the world) used to think they had a "personal relationship" with God... they "felt" God, and they were convinced of the power of prayer. Some were missionaries and clergymen because they wanted to do God's work and some were simply indoctrinated with a religion while they were too young to think for themselves. Some people have switched religions — feeling the "power" of Allah and Jesus and other deities in one lifetime but now they know that there is no personal relationship because there's nothing there. They came to the conclusion that prayer doesn't affect the external world; and they realized that any feelings created by the religion came from within and not from some external source.

Q: Can't God and religion coexist with science?

A: One would first have to define the "God" in question. There are millions of proposed deities that span across cultures and regions throughout human history. I wouldn't necessarily say that every god is fundamentally anti-science except in that they are all based on faith, which is by definition lacking the evidence that science could measure; belief in gods is directly opposed to scientific thought in that way. That being said, if you define God as the Abrahamic God with its affiliated holy texts — the prayer-answering Creator-God who is said to have spoken everything into existence and who supposedly interferes regularly with affairs on earth — then that God is certainly contrary to our progressing scientific understandings. A lot of the conflict between religion and science stems from the stagnancy of scripture; when the Bible is supposed to be the divinely inspired Word of God and then it makes ridiculous claims like that man was made from dirt and the earth was created in six days, you get generations of people who fight against our evolving understandings of our origins, often insisting Creationism be taught in pub-lic schools. If you look at the organizations that have con-sistently impeded the progress of science, you'll see that they are most often religious in nature.

Q: You may not be religious, but don't you think our morals come from religion?

A: No, that's a common misconception. I feel sorry for anyone who thinks they need stone tablets to know not to murder because it is simply not the case. What we now call "morality" has evolved — as nearly every physical and social human attribute has — to aid us in survival and, ulti-mately, reproduction. As a social species, ethical behavior within social interactions is necessary for our development. This morality requires that we be guided by a conscience (or "moral sense") — and not by a god or gods. Historically, founders of religions integrated moral prescriptions from their own time period and region into a religion's teachings as a way to emulate moral transcendence. The problem with this is not that the morals taught are inherently bad, but that the "holy books" are stagnant in nature. Over time, our understanding of what is "moral" changes but the words in the Bible, Qur'an, etc. do not to any great degree. Religions hinder our own moral evolution by teaching followers strict adherence to these archaic traditions. Using the Old Testament, it is easy to see how far we have come in that we no longer condone acts that were explicitly accepted (or commanded) during that period, such as the stoning of disobedient children and non-believers. Even in the New Testament, we have in large part outgrown the ideas of subservience of women and the discrimination of homosexuals as "sinners" who should burn in "Hell." It is important to understand that religions as moral guides can be quite dangerous once those morals are no longer relevant, especially when those "morals" teach discrimination against those who disagree. When all is said and done, the stagnant morals of any holy book will always work to inhibit our own moral evolution over time.

Q: What about the therapeutic benefits of religion?

A: I don't think religion is therapeutic at all, but it certainly doesn't accomplish anything that secular therapies cannot. The mentality that religion instills, while arguably "comforting" at times, does not help the believer solve his or her problems. Religion gives the illusion of therapy while actually shifting responsibilities for outcomes from the person to an unknowable deity — allowing any event to be chalked up to "God's Plan." When a believer accomplishes something great and credits his or her accomplishments to a god, it takes away from the individual's hard work that is likely responsible and implies that person was somehow more important to God than anybody else who may have prayed equally and failed. And, when a believer does something bad, religion grants salvation based solely on belief — allowing "divine" justification for any crime based solely on the unsubstantiated idea that faith forgives sins. "This life is only a test" is a counter-productive mindset; it encourages wishful thinking toward and elusive and likely non-existent afterlife while often enabling the believer to squander this life as somehow less important.

Q: Isn't raising your children as atheists a form of religious indoctrination?

A: Since atheism is not a religion, the simple answer is "no." But I wouldn't raise my children as atheists, although I expect that they would reach that conclusion on their own. I think it is important to give children a healthy dose of religious education early on, teaching them a broad range of comparative mythology and religion from a phenomenological approach. If you study comparative religion, it is harder to be religious because religions are all very similar at the fundamental level. Each organization has similar cult beginnings and "prophets," they each began as local and cultural myths before being applied to a global context, and they are almost always spread through a combination of violence and proselytization. By learning about the origins of myths and the histories of various religious institutions, children can see all religions as part of the same phenomenon, and not see one as inherently superior to all others.

Q: Aren't you just making science your God? Don't you have "faith" that science will always provide the right answers?

A: There is no room for faith in science. Literally defined as "belief without evidence," faith is the antithesis of the scientific method. In science, one is always looking for evidence, verifying data, and updating understandings. Therein lies the clash with most religions and science — the religious put their faith in a book or a teaching that claims transcendence, yet never lives up to it. Scientific findings are not always right, and that is thoroughly recognized. Actually, it is one of the best parts of how scientific understandings work because they are able to be changed and revised when a better idea comes along — scientists don't proclaim a hypothesis to be too "sacred" to be criticized and altered for better results. I don't have faith that science can provide all the answers because "science" already has the answers — the realities are there, we just have to discover them. We are far from done learning new things about the universe, but the moment you give up and have "faith" that some unknowable deity is responsible for everything is the moment that scientific curiosity and intellectual discovery are lost.

Q: If there is a Heaven, would you want to go? Are you afraid that Hell might be real?

A: Heaven and Hell are logically flawed concepts. If you put an "eternity" into perspective, it is hard to imagine that where we supposedly go for an infinite period of time is based solely upon our actions (and beliefs) in a period of usually less than 100 years on earth. Infinite torture in Hell for any trespass on earth is unjustified. As a result of this logical conclusion and the fact that no evidence exists for any type of afterlife, I no more fear the Christian Hell than a Christian fears the Muslim Hell. However, if Heaven and Hell are real and belief in Jesus is the only determining factor as to who is "saved," then Heaven would be a haven for repented rapists and murderers. Not only would Heaven be home to some of the worst criminals in human history, but it would also be an eternity of deity-worship apart from every person who held differing religious beliefs, even if that person was someone you loved deeply for your entire life. I don't want any part of that paradise.

Q: If you aren't religious, why do you spend so much time talking about and studying religion?

A: I've never been a religious person, but I've always been interested in why people believe the things they do. And I find religion — as a phenomenon — very interesting. I've always enjoyed learning about comparative mythology, and modern mythologies are no different. Through an education in Religious Studies, I learned about the creation myths from various cultures and those myths' earlier influences, about the similarities and inconsistencies within each belief system, and how each religion has grown — through a combination of violence and proselytization — from a localized cult to its modern global equivalent. The problems begin when believers try to force their superstitions and beliefs on others, either institutionally or through violence. While extremists kill and die in the name of their religion, so-called moderates fight for legislation to include Creationism in textbooks and, in America, work tirelessly to turn an explicitly secular nation into a Christian one. When believers use their religion as a tool to manipulate the education of children and destroy separation of Church and State, it is absolutely imperative that secular advocates do their part.

Q: By talking about your atheism, aren't you pushing it on others? Why be vocal about it at all?

A: There is nothing wrong with talking about the fact that you're an atheist, and questions like this are oddly reminiscent of questions asked of homosexuals who are "too open" about who they are. Saying, "I'm an atheist" is no more confrontational than the religious identifiers used by believers. For example, in America, we have an abundance of all things Christian, from door-to-door missionaries, mega churches, and WWJD bumper stickers to Ichthys (Jesus Fish) and crucifixes on the necks of men, women, and children — people proclaim, "I'm a Christian!" in more ways than I can count. Unfortunately for me and many atheists, theism and religiosity are the assumed points of view in many cultures and vocal disagreement with the status quo often results in discrimination. Atheists aren't the ones knocking on doors selling their particular brand of "Truth." Atheists don't have massive tax-exempt organizations with influential political action committees dedicated to atheism. And, most importantly, atheists don't insist that everyone who disagrees with them will burn in Hell for eternity.

Q: God is like the wind... you can't see it, but you know it exists. Why do you believe in wind and not God?

A: I don't believe in gods not because they're invisible, but because there's absolutely no evidence of any earthly object or force that points directly to any Supreme Being — or for anything supernatural, for that matter. God is not like the wind — we can clearly and accurately measure the routes of wind patterns and, when winds become potentially dangerous by forming severe weather systems, we can see the wind's movements and understand the forces that generate them. We can feel its forces and scientifically understand why they are there. If I notice a tree is blown over into the road after a storm, I may conclude that the wind is to blame — but there is no action that can be attributed to a "God." There exists chance and good outcomes and bad outcomes, but no outcomes that need be attributed to acts of God. "God's" force is nothing like wind because there is no force to describe.

Q: Why do you do what you do? What is the point of advocating for secularism?

A: I think that we can make a legitimate difference by showing closet non-believers that they're not alone and by educating the religious about the flaws and negative impacts of the belief systems that they've (often unwittingly) dedicated their lives to. Some people spend their entire lives devoted to a religion that claims to be the 'right' religion... they often deny scientific evidence that contradicts their archaic holy books, they sometimes oppress those who disagree with them, and they always do what they do in the name of an unknowable deity... but sometimes, they wake up. Occasionally, they realize that all religions are man-made and that none of them are 'right.' And when they do, they can live happy and fulfilling lives without dogma and without anticipating or fearing an afterlife. If I can play any small role in the process of helping people to live a more honest life, then I've done my job.

Q: If you don't believe in God, what's the meaning of life?

A: In my opinion, the only constant in life — including non-human life — the only objective "meaning" is the innate urge to protect and preserve one's own blood line. That being said, as an atheist, I don't claim to know an over-arching "Meaning of Life." I think that life is only what you make of it. I operate under the understanding that this life shouldn't be lived under the pretense that it is simply a "test" propagated by an invisible, intangible, Creator-God. And it should not be spent identifying with religious traditions and organized groups that, historically, have been at the root of a tremendous amount of oppression and violence. It is my sincere opinion that our precious time on earth should not be spent attempting to justify unbelievable acts of cruelty, death, and disease as a part of "God's Plan" or the greater good — and clinging to ancient texts that preach ill-concealed bigotry and sexism. Instead, we should find ways to make this life happy and satisfying, without regard to the unknowable nature of an afterlife.

Conclusion

A conclusion is the place where
you got tired of thinking."
— Martin H. Fischer (November 10, 1879 - January 19, 1962)

Being openly non-religious is unreasonably tough in many societies. It seems that, in many areas, faith is thought to trump reason — an idea that, while understandably present in most sacred scriptures, doesn't make sense to many people. And that fact does not make non-believers any more likely to lie, cheat, steal, or murder according to every study. When a person takes offense to someone else's lack of faith — whether as a result of their own insecurities of faith or preconceived notions about "atheists" — if they see in practice that atheism does not affect one's ability to act ethically and maintain a happy and full life, perhaps some of the prejudices will fall away.

I hope that the narratives and advice given in this guide to coming out as a non-believer are helpful for those who may be suffering from persecution as a result of their atheism, but also those who simply want to learn about those who decided to leave faith behind or wish to find and connect with likeminded thinkers. Helping to dispel the myths of non-belief among many religious communities is an important task, and with more people deciding to take the crucial step of declaring their disbelief than ever, believers are likely to see that "atheist" is not synonymous with "Satanist," and that non-believers are not "god-hating sinners." People will start to see that their neighbors or children or dentists don't see evidence for belief in archaic superstitions, so maybe it is not that bad after all.

While this book may not be all one needs to successfully come out as an atheist, I hope that it helps guide non-believers young and old throughout that ongoing process. For me, what helped me most to deal with any instance of religious discrimination was to understand religious mindset and the specific intricacies of religious belief. If you understand the historical and cultural aspects of religion, it can help you to understand not just what people believe, but *why* they believe it, and how they come to be so firmly held in that particular mindset. This understanding, perhaps above all else, can help one to navigate the negative interactions that are all too often part of being openly atheistic.

The fact will always remain that people — more often than not — inherit their religious beliefs from parents or childhood mentors. The familial indoctrination that achieves the startling success rate of religious transmission begins with childhood baptisms, forced participation in religious rituals from a young age, and teaching children who are too young to understand that their religion is the only correct one, and that all others will burn in Hell. Once the child is old enough to think logically about the possible veracity of various religions, it is often too late — the religious instruction has been so successful that the child no longer accepts the possibility that they could be wrong.

There is admittedly a trend in religious practice toward the more liberal versions of the traditions. As discussed in the *Introduction*, in the United States, I've noticed a move toward cultural Christianity. While these people may consider themselves "Christians," it is in name only. They often know very little about the tradition or its origins and

instead identify with it out of cultural familiarity and fear of the unknown. But there are also a separate group of religious people in the world today — they are often pushing back against the liberalization of their religion and the growing secularization of first world nations. These hyper-religious zealots are the terrorists proclaiming Jihad against the Westerners and the fundamentalist Christians bombing abortion clinics. They are advocates for Young Earth Creationism being taught in public schools and preach scripture before science and faith before reason. It is with these individuals that the tide of abuse and discrimination against non-believers is most prominent.

The narratives and stories shared in this work are personal and true testimonies that are intended to aid other individuals who may be facing similar situations. I'd like to sincerely thank our contributors; without them, this work could not provide the wide range of viewpoints on the topic of de-conversion. Whether you've recently deconverted or you've been an atheist for years and never experienced a problem, I hope this guide provided some insight into the views of those non-believers who *are* oppressed, as well as some resources to build a community with individuals who, like you, have decided that the best religion is no religion. In the next chapter, I will provide a list of secular organizations and websites that will be useful to any non-believer.

Resources & Support

*"What spectacle can be more edifying
or more seasonable, than that of Liberty
and Learning, each leaning on the other
for their mutual and surest support?"*
— James Madison (March 16, 1751 - June 28, 1836)

For members of the LGBT community, coming out is an established practice. In fact, there is a lot that atheists can learn from that community regarding when, where, and how to come out. For those who identify as LGBT, for example, there are a host of websites, books, documentaries, social networks, counseling programs, and more to aid in the most difficult aspects of coming out to less-than-understanding family and friends. Some programs include the Human Rights Campaign's Resource Guide[34] and AVERT HIV & AIDS Charity.[35] For non-believers, there are also a variety of support programs, although perhaps not nearly enough. Here I will compile a list of various resources for the non-religious — including blogs, social networks, and advocacy programs, as well as a directory of helpful secular organizations. These resources should be helpful to any non-believer — and not necessarily just those who come from unsupportive or fundamentalist families.

---

34 http://www.hrc.org/resources/entry/resource-guide-to-coming-out
35 http://www.avert.org/coming-out.htm

Secular Advocacy Groups and Organizations

American Atheists: Founded in 1963, American Atheists is an organization laboring for the civil liberties of atheists and the absolute separation of government and religion. The organization was born out of a court case in 1959 by the Murray family that challenged prayer recitation in the public schools, *Murray v. Curlett*. Founded by Madalyn Murray O'Hair, the noted atheist activist, American Atheists is dedicated to working for the civil rights of atheists, promoting separation of state and church, and providing information about atheism.

Website: www.atheists.org
E-mail: info@atheists.org
Physical Headquarters: 225 Cristiani Street, Cranford, NJ 07016
Phone Number: (908) 276-7300

American Humanist Association: The mission of the American Humanist Association is to be a clear, democratic voice for Humanism in the United States, to increase public awareness and acceptance of humanism, to establish, protect, and promote the position of humanists in our society, and to develop and advance humanist thought and action.

Website: www.americanhumanist.org
E-mail: aha@americanhumanist.org
Physical Headquarters: 1777 T Street, NW Washington, DC 20009-7125
Phone Number: (202) 238-9088

Americans United for Separation of Church and State: Americans United (AU) represents members and supporters in all 50 states and is dedicated to preserving the constitutional principle of church-state separation as the only way to ensure religious freedom for all. AU is a 501(c) (3) nonprofit educational organization based in Washington,

D.C. Founded in 1947, Americans United works in the courts, in Congress and state legislatures, at the White House, and in the arena of public opinion.

Website: www.au.org
E-mail: americansunited@au.org
Physical Headquarters: 1301 K Street NW, Suite 850E, Washington, DC 20005
Phone Number: (202) 466-3234

Atheist Alliance International: The mission of Atheist Alliance International (AAI) is to challenge and confront religious organizations and faith, and strengthen global atheism by promoting the growth and interaction of atheist and free thought organizations in countries and regions around the world, and by undertaking international educational and advocacy projects.

Website: www.atheistalliance.org
E-mail: info@atheistalliance.org
Physical Headquarters: 1777 T Street NW, Washington, D.C. 20009-7125

Center for Inquiry: New York-based Center for Inquiry (CFI) is a nonprofit educational organization. The mission of the Center for Inquiry is to foster a secular society based on science, reason, freedom of inquiry, and humanist values. Established in 1991 by philosopher and author *Paul Kurtz*, CFI has more than 18 branches in the United States and 39 worldwide.

Website: www.centerforinquiry.net
E-mail: info@centerforinquiry.net
Physical Headquarters: 3965 Rensch Road, Amherst, NY 14228
Phone Number: (716) 636-4869

Coalition of Reason: The United Coalition of Reason is a nonprofit national organization that helps local non-theistic groups work together to achieve higher visibility, gain more members, and have a greater impact in their local areas.

Website: www.unitedcor.org
E-mail: Info@UnitedCoR.org
Physical Headquarters: 1777 T Street, NW Washington, D.C. 20009
Phone Number: (202) 550-9964

Foundation Beyond Belief: Georgia-based Foundation Beyond Belief is a 501(c) (3) charitable foundation created to focus, encourage, and demonstrate humanist generosity and compassion. They select and feature five charitable organizations per quarter, one in each of the following cause areas: Education, Poverty and Health, Human Rights, The Natural World, and Challenge the Gap (charities based in other worldviews).

Website: www.foundationbeyondbelief.org/about
E-mail: www.foundationbeyondbelief.org/contact
Physical Headquarters: P.O. Box 4882, Alpharetta, GA 30023
Phone Number: (770) 667-6347

Freedom from Religion Foundation: The Freedom from Religion Foundation (FFRF) promotes the constitutional principle of separation of state and church and educates the public on matters relating to non-theism. Incorporated in 1978 in Wisconsin, the Foundation is a national membership association of more than 17,000 freethinkers: atheists, agnostics and skeptics of any pedigree. The Foundation is a nonprofit, tax-exempt, educational organization under Internal Revenue Code 501(c) (3). FFRF and its staff attorneys act on numerous violations of separation of state and church on behalf of members and the public, including: prayers in public schools, payment of funds for religious purposes, government funding of pervasively sectarian institutions, and the ongoing campaign against civil rights for women, gays, and lesbians led by churches. FFRF is led by Co-presidents Dan Barker and Annie Laurie Gaylor. Barker is a former minister, evangelist and secular author. Gaylor is an author and executive editor of *Freethought Today*.

Website: www.ffrf.org
E-mail: www.ffrf.org/about/contact/press
Physical Headquarters: PO Box 750, Madison WI 53701
Phone Number: (608) 256-8900

The Military Association of Atheists and Freethinkers: The Military Association of Atheists and Freethinkers (MAAF) is a community support network that connects military members from around the world with each other and with local organizations. In addition to community services, they take action to educate and train both the military and civilian community about atheists in the military and the issues that they face. Where necessary, MAAF identifies, examines, and responds to insensitive practices that illegally promote religion over non-religion within the military or unethically discriminate against minority religions or differing beliefs. MAAF supports Constitutional State-Church Separation and 1st Amendment rights for all service members.

Website: www.militaryatheists.org
E-mail: community@militaryatheists.org
Physical Headquarters: 1380 Monroe St NW PMB 505, Washington, D.C., 20010
Phone Number: (202) 656-MAAF (6223)

Recovering from Religion: Recovering from Religion is a nonprofit organization dedicated to providing multi-dimensional support and encouragement to individuals leaving their religious affiliations through the establishment, development, training, and educational support of local groups nationwide.

Website: www.recoveringfromreligion.org
E-mail: darrelray@thegodvirus.net
Physical Headquarters: Bonner Springs, Kansas, USA
Phone Number: www.recoveringfromreligion.org/pages/contact

Secular Coalition for America: The Secular Coalition for America is a 501(c) (4) advocacy organization whose purpose is to amplify the diverse and growing voice of the non-theistic community in the United States. The Coalition is located in Washington, D.C.

Website: www.secular.org/history
E-mail: www.secular.org/contact
Physical Headquarters: 1012 14th St. NW #205, Washington, D.C. 20005
Phone Number: (202) 299-1091

The Secular Student Alliance: The mission of the Secular Student Alliance is to organize, unite, educate, and serve students and student communities that promote the ideals of scientific and critical inquiry, democracy, secularism, and human-based ethics. The Secular Student Alliance is a 501(c) (3) educational nonprofit. The group works to organize and empower non-religious students around the country.

Website: www.secularstudents.org
E-mail: ssa@secularstudents.org
Physical Headquarters: 1550 Old Henderson Rd. Suite S150, Columbus, OH 43220
Phone Number: (614) 441-9588

Shops

The Arrogant Atheist: A destination for atheist shirts and accessories. Also features an established atheist-themed blog and discussion forum. *www.thearrogantatheist.com*

Atheist Gear: Founded in 2008 as a means to sell a line of atheist quote t-shirts, Atheist Gear has since become a portal to distribute religion-free news, share links, and entertain free-thinkers. *www.atheistgear.net*

EvolvFISH: A Colorado-based enterprise that is dedicated to countering the destructive aspects of religious zealotry. They create and gather enlightened symbols and materials and advertise these products online, focusing on areas where zealots are trying to usurp the freedoms of the targets of their bigotry. *www.evolvefish.com*

The Secular Store: The Secular Writings of David G. McAfee online store. Each item in this store helps promote a secular lifestyle – while injecting some humor into the discourse. *www.cafepress.com/davidgmcafee*

GodSwill Ministries: *Religion is Not of Rational Thought* and *Heretic* clothing and gear available as part of GodSwill Ministries. *www.godswillchurch.com/store*

Social/Political Groups

The OUT Campaign: Richard Dawkins' project that encourages atheists to "come out." The OUT Campaign allows individuals to let others know they are not alone. It can also be a nice way of opening a conversation and help demolish the negative stereotypes of atheists. Let the world know that we are not about to go away and that we are not going to allow those that would condemn us to push us into the shadows. *www.outcampaign.org*

Freethought Books Project: The Freethought Books Project has been donating secular and freethinking literature to inmates, mental hospitals, and others in need since 2005. http://www.freethoughtbooks.org

Godless Americans Political Action Committee: Mobilizing America's non-believers for political activism. *www.godlessamericans.org*

The Humanist Society: Lists celebrants who conduct secular wedding, naming, and death ceremonies. *www.humanist-society.org*

The James Randi Educational Foundation: The James Randi Educational Foundation (JREF) was founded in 1996 to help people defend themselves from paranormal and pseudoscientific claims. The JREF offers a still-unclaimed million-dollar reward for anyone who can produce evidence of paranormal abilities under controlled conditions. Through scholarships, workshops, and innovative resources for educators, the JREF works to inspire this investigative spirit in a new generation of critical thinkers. *www.randi.org*

National Atheist Party: National Atheist Party (NAP) is a U.S. nonprofit 527 political organization formed by atheists, resolved to advance the political ideals of atheists. They seek to politically represent U.S. atheists and all who share the goal of a secular government by gathering the political strength of secularists nationwide while being guided by the values of secular humanism and evidenced-based reasoning. *www.USANAP.org*

Podcasts/Shows

The Atheist Experience: A weekly cable access and online TV show from Austin, Texas geared toward a non-theist audience. *www.atheist-experience.com*

Dogma Debate: Dogma Debate is a live Internet radio show and podcast available on iTunes, Spreaker, and many other listening applications. The show was designed as a platform for discussing controversial religious topics, political issues, current events, gay rights, and feminism. The show encourages conservatives and religious leaders to join the discussion and defend their positions amid the skepticism. *www.dogmadebate.com*

The Imaginary Friends Show: A podcast by atheists for everyone. Imaginary Friends is a social commentary on social commentary, with news, reviews, special guests, Psychic Bob, and Conversations with God. *www.imaginaryfriendsshow.com*

The Infidel Guy: A call-in radio show featuring live webcasts and podcasting. Reginald Vaughn Finley, Sr. and guests discuss philosophy, atheism, theology, the paranormal, science, and evolution. *www.infidelguy.com*

Skepticality: The official podcast of The Skeptics Society and Skeptic Magazine promoting science and critical thinking. *www.skepticality.com*

Skeptically Speaking: Skeptically Speaking interviews researchers, authors and experts to help listeners understand the evidence, arguments, and science behind what's in the news and on the shelves. *www.skepticallyspeaking.ca*

The Thinking Atheist: The Thinking Atheist is a weekly podcast that airs Tuesdays at 6:00 P.M. US/Central time. The host of the podcast is Seth Andrews, a former Christian of 30 years (and former religious broadcaster). *www.thethinkingatheist.com*

Social Networks/Atheist Dating Sites

Atheist Dating Service: Atheist Dating Service is the fastest growing co-operative of online-dating sites in the world. *www.atheistdatingservice.com*

Atheist Passions: You have a better chance of finding Waldo on this site than you do of finding God! Atheist Passions is a free online dating & social networking site specifically for freethinking singles, either Atheist or Agnostic. *www.atheistpassions.com*

Atheist Nexus: The world's largest coalition of non-theists and non-theist communities. *www.atheistnexus.org*

AtheistSocial: A social network for atheists, secular humanists, and freethinkers. *www.atheistsocial.com*

Freethinker Match: A dating website for freethinkers with more than 15,000 members. *www.freethinkermatch.com*

Think Atheist: A community, social networking, and news site focused on bringing free thinkers together and breaking misconceptions about atheism. *www.thinkatheist.com*

Religious Literacy

Blessed Atheist Bible Study: Atheist Bible Study provides "a reading of the bible to see what it actually contains with as few preconceptions as possible." *www.blessedatheist.com*

The Skeptic's Annotated Bible: The Skeptic's Annotated Bible includes the entire text of the King James Version of the Bible in which passages are highlighted that are an embarrassment to the Bible-believer, and the parts of the Bible that are never read in any Church, Bible study group, or Sunday School class are emphasized. The contradictions and false prophecies show that the Bible is not inerrant; the cruelties, injustices, and insults to women are neither good nor just. *www.skepticsannotatedbible.com*

Teaching about Religion: Teaching about Religion provides academic information and teaching materials related to teaching about religion in public schools in support of an educational commitment to pluralism, acknowledgment that public schools are for students of all worldviews, and the professional understanding that public school teachers need to exercise a scrupulous neutrality regarding religion. *www.teachingaboutreligion.com*

Blogs/News Websites

Atheist Blogroll: The Atheist Blogroll is a service provided to the atheist and agnostic blogging community. The blogroll currently maintains over 1,425 blogs. Membership is limited to atheist and agnostic bloggers. *www.atheistblogroll.blogspot.com*

Dangerous Talk: Dangerous Talk is a blog discussing the three most dangerous topics of polite conversation: Religion, Politics, and Sex. Their goal is to fight back against the Religious Right and push for a more free society. *www.dangeroustalk.net*

Ethical Atheist: World events, history, science, and general articles from an atheist's point of view. *www.ethicalatheist.com*

Friendly Atheist: Friendly Atheist is a blog by Hemant Mehta, blogger, math teacher, and author of *I Sold My Soul on eBay. www.patheos.com/blogs/friendlyatheist*

Godless Living: A page dedicated to living a happy life without gods. Topics include Free thought, Humanism, Atheism, Agnosticism, and all forms of non-theism. *http://godlessliving.wordpress.com*

Greta Christina's Blog: Greta Christina has been writing professionally since 1989 on topics including atheism, sexuality and sex-positivity, LGBT issues, politics, culture, and whatever crosses her mind. *http://freethoughtblogs.com/greta*

Positive Atheism: Discusses the history, ethics, and philosophies of atheism. *www.positiveatheism.org*

The Secular Compass: A website hosted by The Way I See it Podcast, the Secular Compass contains a pool of resources to help guide those who may benefit from useful advice and information on secular issues while on their path from belief to non-belief. *www.seeitpodcast.com*

The Secular Web: Online community of non-believers dedicated to the pursuit of knowledge, understanding and tolerance. *www.infidels.org*

The Secular Writings of David G. McAfee: This is my own blog where I share secular articles, essays, and ideas. *www.DavidGMcAfee.com*

Magazines

American Atheist Magazine: A publication by American Atheists, AA Magazine is currently edited by Pamela Whissel. The organization was founded by Madalyn Murray O'Hair.

Canadian Freethinker Magazine: Founded in early 2007, Canadian Freethinker is a quarterly Canadian volunteer-driven magazine that provides a forum for freethinkers across the country and promotes humanist groups and events.

Skeptical Inquirer: Skeptical Inquirer a magazine for the Committee of Skeptical Inquiry. *www.csicop.org/publications*

CPSIA information can be obtained at www.ICGtesting.com
Printed in the USA
LVOW04s1924120914

403837LV00012B/262/P